"Haiti, Return to God"

Bitol Odule

The problem of Haiti is not social or material, but spiritual.

Apostle Odule Bitol

PROVISIONS **PUBLISH**

PROVISIONS PUBLISH LLC

Dedication

I dedicate this book to the Haitian nation and all the other nations that are facing the same problems and are seeking for solutions. I recommend they choose the same path that God has allowed me to take as I strive to guide my nation to return to God.

Look unto me, and be ye saved, all the ends of the earth: for I am God, and there is none else. (Isaiah 45:22)

Table of Contents

Chapter 1 - The Problems of Haiti 21
   a) Corrupt Leadership 24
   b) Weaknesses of Our Judicial System 34
   c) Setting Aside Our Youth 39
   d) Protecting Our Children................................42
   e) Sentimental Influence 46

Chapter 2 – The Origin of Haiti 53
   a) The People Corrupted Themselves 60
   b) A Kingdom Divided Cannot Stand 63
   c) Haiti In Service to Satan 67
   d) A Trumpet Is Blown.....................................70

Chapter 3 - Similarities Between
Israel and Haiti...77
   a) Ingratitude to God 78
   b) Consequence of Disobedience to God.........84
   c) The Truth Will Set Us Free 93

Chapter 4 - Haiti Return to God 99
   a) What Is the truth? 100
   b) Haiti, Wake Up 104

Chapter 5 – A More Excellent Way 113
   a) Be Responsible and Repent 117
   b) Stand United 119
   c) A More Excellent Way 122

Chapter 6 - Participation and Objective..........127
   a) We Are All Guilty 127
   b) Let's Move Toward the Same Goal 130
   c) Attitude for Success 133

Chapter 7 - The True Leader 139
   a) Characteristics of a True Leader 142

Conclusion 147

Plan of Salvation 151

Foreword

*O*n January 12, 2010, Haiti was struck by a powerful earthquake that left more than 220,000 people dead, 300,000 injured, and millions displaced.

Undoubtedly, the Haitian nation has suffered more than any other country in this hemisphere since its momentous declaration of independence in January of 1804. As only the second country in the Americas and the first Latin American country to proclaim its independence, it has had to deal with a steady stream of major obstacles over its more than 200 years of republican history. This nation has had to overcome slavery, war, dictatorships, floods, epidemics, earthquakes, and political struggles among other evils since it proclaimed its independence.

In this book, Apostle Bitol deals with such timely topics as the important role our youth will play in our modern society, and why we must give them opportunities for academic preparation. They are the future of our country and are very instrumental its development. There will be no future development without properly educating the next generation of leaders.

Apostle Bitol also addresses such crucial and controversial issues as, "The Weaknesses of Our Judicial System" and "Haiti In Service to Satan." Both issues are deeply imbedded in the fabric of this nation. Haiti's poor and dispossessed suffer daily as their rights are suppressed due to the inequality and corruption that permeates the judicial system. The author states categorically that much of this nation's suffering is the result of the practice of witchcraft, zombification, animal and human sacrifices, and other unspeakable acts committed against God.

With these and many other topics, the author of "Haiti, Return to God" confronts the issues that have kept the Haitian people in spiritual slumber for more than 200 years. His desire is to awaken the Haitian people to God's truth as he quotes Ephesians 5:14, "Awake, O sleeper, and arise from the dead, and Christ shall shine (make day dawn) upon you and give you light" (AMP).

As you read through this book, you will find the answers to many of the problems regarding the condition of this nation. One thing is sure, Apostle Bitol has found the way to the right answer through his analysis of the Word of God.

Ask God to open your eyes and heart as you read this book, and then pray for the people of Haiti. Pray that Christ will shine His light on Haiti that they might return to God and away from darkness.

-Lorenzo Mota King
Director Executive Social Service of Churches of the Dominican Republic
Shepherd Christian Church of the Community

Prologue

*W*e are truly living the gospel in a more revolutionary phase then any other time in the past four decades. God is pouring out revival in His people and great things are happening. The Spirit of God is touching the hearts of men who seek Him with a sincere heart, and we rejoice in the revelation of His glory.

I have the privilege and opportunity to introduce this magnificent book, written by my brother and friend in the faith, Odule Bitol. I met him many years ago in Tampa, Florida. God has forged a spiritual unity between us that through the years has been able to grow and flourish to the point that we walked together in many aspects of the sharing of the gospel. He's been a great help, counselor, and guide to me in all aspects of my life.

He is a man of character, while at the same time exhibiting a gentle and submissive spirit. He has answered God's call to write about the problems of his country at a very critical time in their history.

These are times of deep crisis and I believe Apostle Bitol has truly focused in on the reality and the origin of all the problems of Haitian people with a cry for them to open their eyes and return to God for their salvation and deliverance.

This call is for the Haitian people to wake up and see the real reason behind their problems so they can help bring about real social change and economic development. He takes the reader back to the origin of these people to try and help us understand the true source of the problems. As he brings the reader from Haiti's beginnings to the present day reality of the crisis situation in this nation, it will become clear that by departing from the principles and rules established in the Word of God, they have brought many of the problems on themselves.

His deep love and concern for his people has lead him to present the need for every Haitian man and woman to refocus on serious study of the Bible, experience a personal encounter with the one true God, and help bring lasting change to this beautiful nation.

He does a masterful job of comparing the biblical accounts of the people of Israel with the people of Haiti. By showing the weaknesses and errors of the people of Israel in the Old Testament and comparing them to the Haitian problems of today, he reinforces his belief that, *the problem of Haiti is not social or material, but spiritual*.

Through thorough analysis and comparison with the Word of God, he shows us that this nation must unite in mind and spiritual so that changes can occur.

This revelation will help all other nations that have been addressing their problems in the wrong way as well.

Through these pages you will see the real reason why the Haitian people have suffered so much. You can contribute in the most simple and effective way to help the Haitian people truly overcome their spiritual blindness—prayer.

The revelation received by Bitol comes at a crucial point in the history of the Haitian people. I'm confident this book will provide practical assistance to anyone who has a heart to see true transformation in not only Haiti but other countries that face similar spiritual battles. Just as God inspired great men like Paul, Peter, Luke, and John to write under the inspiration of the Holy Spirit, He continues to inspire the hearts of those like Apostle Bitol who seek Him with a sincere heart. That is precisely why this book has been written and given to us as an instrument of transformation and change.

I cannot close without thanking Apostle Bitol for giving me the privilege of introducing this book. May God richly bless and abundantly use these pages to spearhead a transforming revolution within the hearts of the Haitian people. I add my sincere and deepest desires to those of Apostle Bitol when I too exhort the people of Haiti to return to God. Amen

-*Rafael L. Almonte*, Pastor

Introduction

*T*he problem of our nation is not social or material. There is always a logical way to deal with social and material problems. However, when a nation ignores and rejects the greatness of God, the consequences that enter into the social and the material conditions of that country cause it to fall into ruin. The problem we must deal with to bring about true change in our country is not without but within us. Each day, as we look around at what is happening, it is clear to see that our nation is moving backward instead of forward.

There is no doubt that many people have expressed an interest in helping Haiti deal with the crisis in our social and economic conditions. I must truly thank all other nations that have good intentions and have offered to help the Haitian people. However, since we are still floundering in the same disappointing conditions, we must ascertain that we have not truly dealt with the root cause of our problems. Once we discover it, what must we do to solve it?

This book is the result of my search for the answer. I propose the answers we seek are found in God's Word. I will help you to see what is happening in our culture is a result of turning away from God. Therefore the solution can only be found by turning back to God.

God tells us through His Word, the Bible, we must forget the past, but at the same time He wants us to learn lessons from the past. The Holy Spirit has opened my understanding and taught me how to help those who are being destroyed for lack of the knowledge about the one true God through the life of the Prophet Jonah. He has shown me that a servant of the Lord is not supposed to be selfish, but to serve all those who God has placed in his or her path without exception.

My dear brothers and sisters, God has selected this particular moment to plant a seed of knowledge into your life. He desires to teach you how to face the challenge that is ahead of you. God has caused me to care about what you are facing and the oppression you are going through in your life. God wants to let you know that no matter what you are going through in your life right now, the answer you have been looking for is right beside you.

But the word is very near you, in your mouth and in your heart, that you may do it. (Deuteronomy 30:14 NKJV)

God is telling you today:

Seek ye the Lord while he may be found, call ye upon him while he is near. (Isaiah 55:6)

Starting today, I want you to stand up and fight for what you believe is right for your life. I pray that as you do, Almighty God will watch over your life and guide your steps everywhere you go.

I thank God with all my heart for inspiring me to write this book. I believe with all my heart that everyone who reads the truths He has called me to share will be inspired to join me in this grand project that God has laid on my heart for the people of Haiti. As I share the history of this nation, I pray all will recognize the need for the people of Haiti to turn their hearts back to God.

Father God, Creator of heaven, earth, sea, and all things therein, I ask You in the name of Jesus to please give understandings to all of those who read this book for the good of our country. Amen!

Now read with a fresh mind as I share about my country and its people. May God bless you in His infinite love and reveal to you His irrefutable truths.

-Apostle Odule Bitol

God Have Mercy on Haiti

Unto thee lift I up mine eyes, O thou that dwells in the heavens. Behold, as the eyes of servants look unto the hands of their masters, and as the eyes of a maiden unto the hand of her mistress; so our eyes wait upon the Lord our God, until that we have mercy upon us. Have mercy upon us, O Lord, have mercy upon us: for we are exceedingly filled with contempt. Our soul is exceedingly filled with the scorning of those that are ease, and with the contempt of the proud. (Psalm 123)

Chapter One

The Problems of Haiti

*P*overty affects the Haitians in many aspects of everyday life, including housing, nutrition, education, healthcare, infant mortality rates, as well as the environment. Haiti has constantly been plagued with low levels of living conditions. Since its independence, Haiti has had difficulties of all kinds and at all levels. Whether social, political, economic, educational, or religious, the leaders that have governed us have never taken responsibility and never sought to identify the fundamental problems of this nation.

Therefore is judgment far from us, neither doth justice overtake us: we wait for light, but behold obscurity; for brightness, but we walk in darkness. (Isaiah 59:9)

Matthew Henry's Concise Commentary explains, "If we shut our eyes against the light of Divine truth, it is just with God to hide from our eyes the things that belong to our peace. The sins of those who profess themselves God's people are worse than the sins of others. **And the sins of a nation bring public judgments, when not restrained by public justice. Men may murmur under calamities, but nothing will truly profit while they reject Christ and his gospel.**"[1]

Our people can murmur and complain about the condition of our economy and the injustice done to the poor, but if as a nation we shut our eyes to God and remain in spiritual slumber, nothing will truly change for the good.

The Apostle Paul gives us insight into this as he instructs "nations" in the New Testament who failed to overcome adversity because they lacked one very important thing.

> **Our leaders have never sought to identify the fundamental problems of this nation.**

*Destruction and misery are in their ways: And the way of peace have they not known: **There is no fear of God before their eyes.*** (Romans 3:16-18)

The fear of God referred to in this scripture means the "reverential awe of Him who would chasten and lift the soul out of its deepest depressions; but to all this the natural man is a stranger."[2] When man refuses to have a reverential fear of God, he will be pulled toward a path of destruction which never leads to peace and joy.

> But **in every nation** he who venerates and **has a reverential fear for God**, treating Him with worshipful obedience and living uprightly, **is acceptable to Him** and sure of being received and welcomed [by Him]. (Acts 10:35 AMP)

God blesses those nations whose people show reverential fear toward His ways and seek to obey His laws. When a nation chooses to put money or power before God, it shall not prosper. Without God's blessing, a nation is left unguarded and is subject to any greater power. They will inevitably end up in bondage to whatever power gains dominance. We are warned in God's Word that we cannot successfully serve two masters.

> No servant is able to serve two masters; for either he will hate the one and love the other, or he will stand by and be devoted to the one and despise the other. You cannot serve God and mammon (riches, or anything in which you trust and on which you rely). (Luke 16:13 AMP)

You may ask me how has Haiti shown that it is not serving God. That is the question we must answer if we are to uncover the root problem for all the difficulties our nation has experienced. Once we can expose the areas that displease God, we can make the changes necessary to begin to receive God's bless-ings on our people and our land.

> ***If my people***, *which are called by my name*, ***shall humble themselves, and pray, and seek my face, and turn from their wicked ways;*** *then will I hear from heaven, and will forgive their sin, and* ***will heal their land***. (2 Chronicles 7:14)

God has clearly stated how we can begin to receive the blessings of heaven upon our land and our people. Let us dig deeper into the areas where we have not been people who are called by His name. As we discover areas of disobedience or lack of reveren-tial fear of God, let us begin to pray and seek His face to help our nation turn from its wicked ways and call upon God to heal our land.

Corrupt Leadership

My brothers, think of how you feel you when you see somebody mistreat one of your Haitians brothers. I feel the same way. But it pains me even more when I see brother mistreat brother. We are supposed to watch over one another not make slaves out of those who are incapable of caring for themselves by taking advantage of their poverty to

> **Our leaders have never set up a structure for the training and equipping of the next generation.**

24

gain what we want from them. Until we begin to do this our country will never be able to move forward in prosperity for all.

> *Now therefore, it is already an utter failure for you that you go to law against one another. Why do you not rather accept wrong? Why do you not rather let yourselves be cheated? No, you your-selves do wrong and cheat, and you do these things to your brethren.* (1 Corinthians 6:7-8 NKJV)

Haiti is facing right at this moment the same thing the Jews were when they returned to rebuild their lives in Jerusalem after their Babylonian exile. We can gain great encouragement from the way God always made a way for His people who turned their hearts back to Him to come out of whatever they were going through and be victorious over every enemy. Look very carefully at what Nehemiah said to the people out of his love for his nation.

> *And I was very angry when I heard their cry and these words. Then I consulted with myself, and **I rebuked the nobles, and the rulers, and said unto them, ye exact usury, everyone of his brother**. And I set a great assembly against them. And I said unto them, we after our ability have redeemed our brethren the Jews, which were sold unto the heathen. And will ye even sell your brethren? Or shall they be sold unto us? Then held them their peace, and found nothing to answer.*

Also I said it is not good that ye do: ought ye not to walk in the fear of our God because of the reproach of the heathen our enemies? I like-wise, and my brethren, and servant, might exact of them money, and corn; I pray you; let us leave off this usury. Restore, I pray you, to them, even this day, their lands, their vineyards, their olive yards, and their houses, also the hundredth part of the money, and of the corn, the wine, and the oil, that ye exact of them. Then said they, we will restore them, and will require nothing of them; so will we do as thou sayest. Then I called the priests, and took an oath of them, that they should do according to this promise. Also I shook my lap, and said, so God shake out every man from his house, and from his labor, that per for meth not this promise, even thus be he shaken out, Amen, and praised the lord. And the people did according to this promise. (Nehemiah 5:6-13)

Now I plead with you my Haitian brothers, if you are among those who have already risen above poverty and want, please give those a chance who have never tasted of a decent life. Stop abusing your own brothers. Because we all come from one blood and we have a unique past. None of us is superior to another, but we are all equal, same language and we live in the same territory. I suggest that we must learn to avoid making the same mistakes of the past. We must develop a different mentality that is based and founded on the word of God. "Jesus said: Love the Lord your God with all your heart and with all your soul and with thy entire mind. This is the first and greatest commandment. And the second is like it: Love your neighbor as yourself. Matthew 22: 37-39»

Nehemiah has given us a valuable example of how we should treat our own people. Nehemiah's words helped me to understand that in all occasions we must give priority to what is right for the sake of the people. Jesus gave us the same commandment as recorded in Luke 17:3-4.

*Pay attention and always be on your guard [**looking out for one another**]. If your brother sins (misses the mark), solemnly tell him so and reprove him, and if he repents (feels sorry for having sinned), forgive him. And even if he sins against you seven times in a day, and turns to you seven times and says, I repent [I am sorry], **you must forgive him (give up resentment and consider the offense as recalled and annulled)**.* (AMP)

Matthew Henry's Concise Commentary says to us, "Christians should not contend with one another, for they are brethren. This, if duly attended to, would prevent many law-suits, and end many quarrels and disputes. In matters of great damage to ourselves or families, we may use lawful means to right ourselves, but Christians should be of a forgiving temper. Refer the matters in dispute, rather than go to law about them. They are trifles, and may easily be settled, if you first conquer your own spirits. Bear and forbear, and the men of least skill among you may end your quarrels. It is a shame that little quarrels should grow to such a head among Christians, that they cannot be determined by the brethren. The peace of a man's own mind, and the calm of his neighborhood are worth more than victory. Lawsuits could not take place among brethren, unless there were faults among them."³

The Apostle Paul instructed the new Christians in his first letter to the Thessalonians concerning how we are to treat our brothers even if they have done evil towards us.

> *Now we exhort you, brethren, warn them that are unruly, comfort the feebleminded, support the weak, be patient toward all men. See that none render evil for evil unto any man; but ever follow that which is good, both among yourselves, and to all men.* (1 Thessalonians 5:14-15)

However, if we see a brother heading down the wrong path, we have a responsibility to help him see the light and bring him back from destruction. "If your brother wrongs you, go and show him his fault, between you and him privately. If he listens to you, you have won back your brother" (Matthew 18:15 AMP).

> *[Therefore **beware**] brethren, take care, lest there be in any one of you a wicked, unbelieving heart [which refuses to cleave to, trust in, and rely on Him], leading you to turn away and desert or stand aloof from the living God. But instead warn*

*(**admonish, urge, and encourage) one another every day**, as long as it is called Today, that none of you may be hardened [into settled rebellion] by the deceitfulness of sin [by the fraudulence, the stratagem, the trickery which the delusive glamor of his sin may play on him].* (Hebrews 3:12-13 AMP)

At the same time when the darkness invades our country, we must condemn it and not cover it up. We must work together to fight this darkness to bring it to light. When we are enlightened it is our responsibility to keep that light shining.

> **When the darkness invades our country, we must condemn it and not cover it up.**

The Apostle Paul warns us against allowing darkness to be allowed to enter and spread among our people.

*For this ye know, that no whoremonger, nor unclean person, nor covetous man, who is an idolater, hath any inheritance in the kingdom of Christ and of God. **Let no man deceive you with vain words: for because of these things cometh the wrath of God upon the children of disobedience.** Be not ye therefore partakers with them. For ye were sometimes darkness, but now are ye light in the Lord: walk as children of light: (For the fruit of the Spirit is in all goodness and righteousness and truth;) Proving what is acceptable unto the Lord. And **have no fellowship with the***

unfruitful works of darkness, but rather reprove them. *For it is a shame even to speak of those things which are done of them in secret. But all things that are reproved are made manifest by the light: for whatsoever doth make manifest is light.* **Wherefore he saith, Awake thou that sleepest, and arise from the dead, and Christ shall give thee light.** (Ephesians 5:5-14)

Matthew Henry's Concise Commentary warns us: "Filthy lusts must be rooted out. These sins must be dreaded and detested. Here are not only cautions against gross acts of sin, but against what some may make light of. But these things are so far from being profitable that they pollute and poison the hearers."[4]

"The devil and the wicked will not suffer themselves to be made manifest by the light, but love darkness, though *outwardly* the light shines round them. Therefore, 'light' has no transforming effect on *them*, so that they do not become light (John 3:19-20). But, says the apostle, you being now light yourselves (Ephesians 5:8), by bringing to light through reproof those who are in darkness, will convert them to light. Your consistent lives and faithful reproofs will be your 'armor of light' (Romans 13:12) in making an inroad on the kingdom of darkness."[5]

What I noticed from our so-called political leaders is that they work for the benefit of themselves and those who are their relatives. They are not working in the favor of our country. They show by their actions that they don't care about Almighty God who is above everything. The sad part is that the One who they don't care about is the One who gave them their position in the first place. Romans 13:1 says, "For there is no power but of God the powers that be are ordained of God."

The politics in Haiti is filled with corruption and is corrupting others.

Thus saith God, Why transgress ye the commandments of the LORD, that ye cannot prosper? Because ye have forsaken the LORD, he hath also forsaken you. (2 Chronicles 24:20b)

In 2009, Haiti was ranked the tenth most corrupt country in the world by Transparency International's Corruption Perception Index, with a CPI score of 1.8. Studies conducted by Transparency International shows a strong correlation between corruption and poverty. Corruption increases poverty through lower economic growth rates, biased tax systems which would also lead to a widening disparity between the rich and the poor, poor

> Our government leaders do not defend the interests of our nation; only that of their egos.

implementation of social programs, lower welfare spending and unequal access to education. Specifically for Haiti, studies have shown that international donors have been slow to assist Haiti, mainly due to widespread corruption and structural problems present in Haiti. Overseas charitable organizations have contributed more than 2.6 billion dollars' worth of aid to the country since 1994, of which any obvious benefits have yet to seen.[6]

A politician or a government official is not supposed to be against the interests of his country, but our government leaders do not defend the interests of our nation; only that of their egos.

> *For from the least of them even unto the greatest of them every one is given to covetousness; and from the prophet even unto the priest every one dealt falsely. They have healed also the hurt of daughter of my people slightly, saying, peace, peace; when there is no peace. When they ashamed when they had committed abomination? Nay, they were not at all ashamed, neither could they blush:* **therefore they shall fall among them that fall: at the time that I visit them they shall be cast down, saith the Lord.** (Jeremiah 6:13-15).

God will never leave evil unpunished. Psalm 37:9 assures us, "For evildoers shall be cut off: but those that wait upon the LORD, they shall inherit the earth." Does that mean we just sit back and let God strike dead our corrupt leadership? No, we are to be Christ's ambassadors and bring God's truth to a corrupt and perverse generation of leadership, and begin to replace the evildoers with those whose desire is to better our nation and serve the one true God.

*So this I say and solemnly testify in [the name of] the Lord [as in His presence], **that you must no longer live as the heathen** (the Gentiles) do in their perverseness [in the folly, vanity, and emptiness of their souls and the futility] of their minds. **Their moral understanding is darkened and their reasoning is beclouded.** [They are] alienated (estranged, self-banished) from the life of God [with no share in it; this is] because of the ignorance (the want of knowledge and perception, the willful blindness) that is deep-seated in them, due to their hardness of heart [to the insensitiveness of their moral nature]. **In their spiritual apathy they have become callous and past feeling and reckless and have abandoned themselves [a prey] to unbridled sensuality, eager and greedy to indulge in every form of impurity [that their depraved desires may suggest and demand].*** (Ephesians 4:17-19 AMP)

We must use wisdom and rely on the power of God to help us not only defend ourselves against being pulled into this corruption, but also fight to eliminate it by speaking the truth in love for, "Whatsoever a man soweth, that shall he also reap" (Galatians 6:7).

How do we do this? Ephesians 4:25-32 gives us a plan of action that involves each of us beginning in our own neighborhoods and areas of influence and then spreading the truth to our towns, cities, and our governmental leaders.

Wherefore putting away lying, **speak every man truth with his neighbour:** *for we are members one of another.* **Be ye angry, and sin not:** *let not the sun go down upon your wrath: Neither give place to the devil. Let him that stole* **steal no more:** *but rather let him labour, working with his hands the thing which is good, that he may have to* **give to him that needeth. Let no corrupt communication proceed out of your mouth,** *but that which is good to the use of edifying, that it may minister grace unto the hearers. And grieve not the holy Spirit of God, whereby ye are sealed unto the day of redemption. Let* **all bitterness, and wrath, and anger, and clamour, and evil speaking, be put away from you,** *with all malice: And* **be ye kind one to another, tenderhearted, forgiving one another,** *even as God for Christ's sake hath forgiven you.*

Weaknesses of Our Judicial System

Haiti ranks 59.5 in the <u>Gini Coefficient</u> index, with the richest 10% of Haitians receiving 47.83% of the nation's income, while the poorest 10% receive less than 0.9%. The government in Haiti is known for running a slow, inefficient and corrupt system of justice. Allegations of torture and kidnapping are common whereas the number of Haitian citizens imprisoned without trial is huge. Lawyers' immunity is under constant threat. Lawyers have been intimidated from defending their clients through pressure and violence. Courts of justice were in effect "run by the judges, appointed by the President for Life" who lacked the independence to make judgments about abuses against human rights.[7]

It's impossible for a country to grow without a strong, stable justice system that functions according to the knowledge of the One who is above every-thing. Justice is rendering to every one that which is his due. It has been distinguished from equity in this respect. While justice means merely the doing what positive law demands, equity means the doing of what is fair and right in every separate case.[8] God gives us specific instructions as to the character of the judicial system should be if we want to receive His blessings and protection over our land.

> God is just. He will never remain in a nation that practices injustice.

You shall appoint judges and officers in all your towns which the Lord your God gives you, according to your tribes, and they shall judge the people with righteous judgment. You shall not misinterpret or misapply judgment; you shall not be partial, or take a bribe, for a bribe blinds the eyes of the wise and perverts the words of the righteous. Follow what is altogether just (uncompromisingly righteous), that you may live and inherit the land which your God gives you. (Deuteronomy 16:18-20 AMP)

God is just. He will never remain in a nation that practices injustice. He tells us very clearly throughout the Bible that He hates a nation that doesn't lead in righteousness. In fact He promises that He will erase them from the surface of the earth, like He wiped the people who were the inhabitants of the country of Canaan before Israel.

That the land spew not you out also, when ye defile it, as it spewed out the nation that were before you. For whosoever shall commit any of these abominations, even the soul that commit them shall be cut off from among their people. (Leviticus 18:28-29)

The Haitian judicial system is fraudulent at all levels among those who are supposed to see that our nation is just in all of its dealings with its people. The Bible warns lawmakers not to develop any legislation that does not benefit the people under their oversight.

Woe unto them that decree unrighteous decrees and that write grievousness which they have prescribed. As lawmakers you need to support the people through your bills, because God will punish those one who do the opposite, And what will ye do in the day of visitation, and in desolation which shall come from far? To whom will ye flee for help? And where will ye leave your glory? Without me they shall bow down under the prisoner and they shall fall under the slain. For all this is anger is not turned away, but his hand is stretched out still. (Isaiah 10:1, 3- 4)

In Haiti we always say that a wooden door cannot fight with the metal door. In our judicial system, I look at the way our courts operate and see that they are just like a black market business. It seems our courts operate for personal gain instead of for truly seeking to meter out righteous judgments. God wants us to give justice to those who deserve justice. Only righteous judges can officiate over our justice system if we truly want to see an increase in our country's economic and social conditions.

Ye shall not respect persons in judgment; but ye shall hear the small as well as the great; ye shall not be afraid of the face of man; for the judgment is God's: and the cause that it too hard for you, bring it unto me, and I will hear it. (Deuteronomy 1:17)

God has told us to guard against any type of injustice in any form whatsoever.

Hearken now unto my voice, I will give you the counsel, and God shall be with thee: be thou for the people to God-ward, that thou mayest bring the causes unto God. (Exodus 18:19)

The prophets of the Old Testament were not only sent to warn the people of impending doom but also give them a chance to change their unjust and evil ways. Jonah was sent to Ninevah and Amos was sent to Israel to warn of God's judgment on their nations if they did not turn from greed and injustice.

"The same almighty power can, for repenting sinners, easily turn affliction and sorrow into prosperity and joy, and as easily turn the prosperity of daring sinners into utter darkness. Evil times will not bear plain dealing; that is, evil men will not. And these men were evil men indeed, when wise and good men thought it in vain even to speak to them. Those who will seek and love that which is good, may help to save the land from ruin. It behoves us to plead God's spiritual promises, to beseech him to create in us a clean heart, and to renew a right spirit within us. The Lord is ever ready to be gracious to the souls that seek him; and then piety and every duty will be attended to. But as for sinful Israel, God's judgments had often passed by them, now they shall pass through them."[9]

> *Therefore because you impose heavy rent on the poor And exact a tribute of grain from them, Though you have built houses of well-hewn stone, Yet you will not live in them; You have planted pleasant vineyards, yet you will not drink their wine. For I know your transgressions are many and your sins are great, You who distress the righteous and accept bribes And turn aside the poor in the gate.* (Amos 5:11-12 NAS)

I truly pray our nation will turn from its evil unjust ways and see that only through turning our minds and hearts back to God can we reverse the disastrous future we are swiftly heading for.

Setting Aside Our Youth –
the Key to Our Future

We cannot always build the future for our youth, but we can build our youth for the future. (Franklin D. Roosevelt)

Education levels in Haiti are low. Haiti's literacy rate of about fifty-three percent falls well below the ninety percent average literacy rate for Latin American and Caribbean countries. The country faces shortages in educational supplies and qualified teachers, and the rural population remains underrepresented in the country's classrooms. Currently, most Haitian schools are private rather than state-funded. Though the Constitution requires that a public education be offered free to all people, the Haitian government has been unable to fulfill this obligation. It spent 10% of government funds for the country's elementary and secondary schools (Wikipedia, the free encyclopedia).

Out of the 67% enrollment rate for elementary school, 70% continue on to the third grade. 60% of all students drop out of school before the sixth grade. One of the reasons is the poor quality of the Haitian education sector. Less than 40% of schools are accredited. 15% of teachers at the elementary level have basic teaching qualifications, including university degrees. Nearly 25% have never even attended secondary school. Many teachers ended up leaving their profession for alternative better paying jobs due to the lack of sufficient government funding as they are either given a meager salary or are not even paid at all (*Wikipedia*, the free encyclopedia).

The education system suffered setbacks from the earthquake in January 2010. According to the United Nations Educational, Scientific and Cultural Organization (UNESCO), Haiti has been facing multiple challenges in the higher education sector. Universities in Haiti lost a significant number of students as the earthquake collapsed and damaged many school buildings and equipment. Such poor and unconducive living conditions within the nation is one important factor contributing to the shortage of skilled labor in the workforce, with an estimated 85% of college-educated Haitians choosing to live abroad.

Consequently, another area where our leaders are receiving and acting on evil destructive counsel is the care and training of our children. Haiti cannot be developed into a strong and prosperous nation without taking into account the training and equipping of our youth who are the key to the future of our nation. I think one of the major problems of our country is the setting aside of our youth. I am convinced that the role of our leaders is to support the youth and help guide them so they will be prepared to be the next generation of leadership. But the reality is I think the training of our youth is not a priority for our leaders.

Why do the heathen rage and the people imagine a vain thing? The kings of the earth set themselves, and the rulers take counsel together, against the LORD, and against his anointed, saying, Let us break their bands asunder, and cast away their cords from us. (Psalm 2:1-3)

Our economy is out of order because our leaders have never set up a structure for the training and equipping of the next generation. The structure that they have put together is to secure everything to be under their control for their own interests for the here and now. However, if the economy is going to move forward we must remove the road blocks that have blocked the way for our youth to grow and prosper. Instead of encouraging and helping our youth to build on what they already have learned in school, I think they have done their best to stop the motor that will drive this country ahead into prosperity from running.

It seems the normal pattern that once a young person has completed their classical studies, instead of making higher education available to them, they are merely released into society to settle for whatever work they can find instead of seeking to use the talents God has placed within them to better our country. Without adequate training programs for our youth, they will become a burden to society instead of being the way to move this country forward economically.

Where no counsel is, the people fall: but in the multitude of counselors there is safety. (Proverbs 11:14)

If we are not providing a way for our youth to attain a higher education, where are they being trained and by whom? Until we upgrade our educational system and provide accredited higher education programs and universities, our youth will either become unproductive adults or they will leave our country to go where they can prosper and grow. We need to build universities and give our youth a chance to use the knowledge and the gifts of God within them to improve conditions in our beautiful country, and become the leaders this country needs to grow and prosper.

> *Blessed is the man that walketh not in the counsel of the ungodly, nor standeth in the way of sinners, nor sitteth in the seat of the scornful. But his delight is in the law of the LORD; and in his law doth he meditate day and night. And he shall be like a tree planted by the rivers of water, that bringeth forth his fruit in his season; his leaf also shall not wither; and whatsoever he doeth shall prosper. (Psalm 1:1-3)*

Protecting Our Children

> *Lo, children are an heritage of the LORD: and the fruit of the womb is his reward.* (Psalm 127:3)

A family that educates their kids from the beginning helps to lead our society in the right direction. The foundation of a nation depends on the strength of its families. Just as it is difficult to face issues of the family without unity and a strong belief and faith in God, a country that doesn't have leadership that fears God will find it very difficult to overcome a crisis whether economical, political or spiritual. For our country to come out of what we are facing now, we have to better understand how we should do things together in unity for the betterment and protection of all of our people, but especially our children.

The high <u>Infant Mortality</u> Rate of sixty-four deaths per 1000 live births is a result of the poor healthcare system, and the lack of a well-planned education system is the cause of low <u>literacy rates</u> (45%) in the country of Haiti (Wikipedia).

"Children are God's gifts, a heritage, and a reward; and are to be accounted blessings, and not burdens: he who sends mouths, will send meat, if we trust in him. They are a great support and defense to a family. Children who are young, may be directed aright to the mark, God's glory, and the service of their generation; but when they are gone into the world, they are arrows out of the hand, it is too late to direct them then."[10]

Jesus Himself warned us in Matthew 18:6, "Whoever causes one of these little ones who believe in Me to sin, it would be better for him if a millstone were hung around his neck, and he were drowned in the depth of the sea" (NKJV).

When a man is properly fathered, he will in turn become a good head of his own household. This same principle holds true in leadership. A leader that was raised in a godly family and was taught to obey God's principles will automatically be a caring and godly leader. He will understand the benefits of meeting the needs of all our country's families no matter what their social or financial station in life.

And ye, fathers, provoke not your children to wrath: but bring them up in the nurture and admonition of Lord. (Ephesians 6:4)

We also need to think about the children that do not have the benefit of a solid family unit to grow up in. In addition to suffering from chronic malnourishment and a lack of educational opportunity, many Haitian children also suffer physical abuse. In 2004 the Ministry of Labor and Social Affairs reported that its hotline received more than 700 calls from children reporting abuse. Few statistics regarding the wider problem of child abuse have been collected. Trafficking of children also is a significant problem. UNICEF estimates that 2,000 to 3,000 Haitian children per year are trafficked (Wikipedia).

> **In addition to suffering from chronic malnourishment and a lack of educational opportunity, many Haitian children also suffer physical abuse.**

What is our government doing to help those who cannot help themselves or are victims of crime that is perpetrated against these unprotected children of our society? What are our leaders doing about the issue of those children who are victims of sexual abuse or human trafficking? Because of the that position that was never truly dealt with God has placed me, I find myself confronting this type of case every day. Recently I received a terrible report of a girl that was raped at the age of eleven by a twenty year old man. She is now seventeen and chose to share the consequences this crime has had on her life with me.

This young girl thanked me for allowing her to bring out all these secrets that had gnawed at her heart for so many years and deal with the issue so she could truly move on with her life. This story touched me deeply as a father of four daughters that I cherish as a true blessing from God. May all the fathers of our country take heed of this warning!

To my horror, I discovered evidence of how some of the officials placed in our government to fight against the trafficking of children from the age of seven to fifteen years have been part of this lusted filled wicked phenomenon. In fact some of those leaders are still in the news for misappropriation of minors. I send out a warning from God who has a plan for all those who do evil especially to our children.

When I say unto the wicked, thou shalt surely die; and thou neither givest him not warning, nor speakest to warn the wicked from is wicked way, to save his life; the same wicked man shall die in is iniquity; but his blood will require at thine hand. Yet if thou warn the wicked, and he turn not from is wickedness, nor from is wicked way, he shall die in his iniquity; but thou has delivered thy soul. (Ezekiel 3:18-19)

Sentimental Influence

Jesus said, let them alone: they are blind, leaders of the blind. And if the blind lead the blind, both shall fall into the ditch. (Matthew 15:14)

Very often we mix our feeling with the reality and if they're mixed we will never see the truth. One of the biggest problems I see causing the break down of our country is the sentimental problem or holding onto the traditions of men. It's time for us to learn how to separate feeling from the reality. Though we do need to feel compassion for our fellowman and care for the widows and orphans, a nation that is governed by emotion cannot prosper. The Bible teaches us how Jesus managed His emotions when his brothers and his mother were looking for him.

Then one said unto him, behold, thy mother and thy brethren stand without, desiring to speak with thee. But he answered and said unto him that told him, who is my mother? And who are my brethren? And he stretched forth his hand toward his disciples, and said, behold my mother and brethren! For whosoever shall do the will of my father which is in heaven, the same is my brother, and sister, and mother. (Mathew 12:47, 50)

Jesus knew that, though He did have an emotional attachment to His family, He had responsibilities as a leader and teacher of God's Law. Was He teaching us not to properly care for our family? No!

46

But He was showing us how to set our priorities. We are to serve God, care for our families, and serve our fellowman. He even warned us there may be times when our family will turn against us when it comes to obedience to the things of God.

In the case recorded in Matthew 12, Jesus was "absorbed in the awful warnings He was pouring forth. He felt this to be an unseasonable interruption, fitted to dissipate the impression made upon the large audience—such an interruption as duty to the nearest relatives did not require Him to give way to. But instead of a direct rebuke, He seizes on the incident to convey a sublime lesson, expressed in a style of inimitable condescension."[11]

King Solomon also showed us that a leader must sometimes put his feelings aside when it comes to ruling a nation with wisdom and justice. At times it is harder to overcome our own passions, than the attacks of an enemy.[12]

He that is slow to anger is better than the mighty; and he that ruleth his spirit than he that taketh a city. (Proverbs 16:32)

To overcome our own passions, requires more steady management, than obtaining victory over an enemy.[13] God want us to learn to react with justice and wisdom!

When the righteous are in authority, the people rejoice: but when the wicked beareth rule, the people mourn. (Proverbs 29:2)

The king by justice establishes the land, but he who exacts gifts and tribute overthrows it. (Proverbs 29:4 AMP)

I have often noticed that the dreams of our leaders are buried by their feelings despite their good intentions. They have to resolve the problems of our country without mixing "feelings with business" because they are two separate issues. What happens when we mix them in an unbalanced way is that it blinds us to the true needs of our country and prevents us from being able to provide for our true needs. I fear that sometimes in an effort to protect our culture and its traditions from outside influence, we miss the opportunities God has given us to better ourselves.

So for the sake of your tradition (the rules handed down by your forefathers), you have set aside the Word of God [depriving it of force and authority and making it of no effect]. (Matthew 15:6 AMP)

> **To overcome our own passions requires more steady management than obtaining victory over an enemy.**

I see an economic model very near to us that has been able to protect the positive sides of their culture and yet improve the economy of their people without compromising their moral standards. When

the Dominican Republic's President Balaguer implemented a wise social and economic plan to invite
select foreign investors to approach their nation, it
facilitated the development of the tourism industry
in his country. It increased monetary flow into his
country and gave his people new means of employ-
ment so they could work to bring themselves out of
poverty. This in turn boosted the economy of the
whole nation.

The Dominican Republic has the second largest
economy in the Caribbean. It is an upper middle-
income developing country primarily dependent on
agriculture, trade, and services, especially tourism.
Although the service sector has recently overtaken
agriculture as the leading employer of Dominicans
(due principally to growth in tourism and Free Trade
Zones), agriculture remains the most important sector
in terms of domestic consumption and is in second
place (behind mining) in terms of export earnings.
Tourism accounts for more than $1 billion in annual
earnings. Free trade zone earnings and tourism are
the fastest-growing export sectors. According to a
1999 International Monetary Fund report, remittances from Dominican Americans, are estimated to
be about $1.5 billion per year. Most of these funds are
used to cover basic household needs such as shelter,
food, clothing, health care, and education. Second-
arily, remittances have financed small businesses and
other productive activities (Wikipedia).

What stops us from implementing a wise economic plan in our country?

> *See to it that no one carries you off as spoil or makes you yourselves captive by his so-called philosophy and intellectualism and vain deceit (idle fancies and plain nonsense), following human tradition (men's ideas of the material rather than the spiritual world), just crude notions following the rudimentary and elemental teachings of the universe and disregarding [the teachings of] Christ (the Messiah).* (Colossians 2:8 AMP)

There is a philosophy which rightly exercises our reasonable faculties; a study of the works of God, which leads us to the knowledge of God, and confirms our faith in him. But there is a philosophy which is vain and deceitful; and while it pleases men's fancies it hinders their faith. Those who walk in the way of the world are turned from following Christ.[14]

This is a warning we must heed as we consider how to improve the conditions of our people; economically, socially, and spiritually. There must be balance in our leadership and they must choose to pursue wisdom from above and not necessarily stay bound by our traditions and emotional attachment to the past. We will investigate how to bring this balance as we study the origins of our beautiful country in the next chapter.

> *Uprightness and right standing with God (moral and spiritual rectitude in every area and relation) elevate a nation, but sin is a reproach to any people.* (Proverbs 14:34 AMP)

What are the root problems of Haiti?

➤ *Our leaders have never sought to identify the fundamental problems of this nation.*

➤ *The politics in Haiti is filled with corruption and is corrupting others.*

➤ *Our leaders have never set up a structure for training and equipping the next generation.*

➤ *In addition to suffering from chronic malnourishment and a lack of educational opportunity, many Haitian children also suffer physical abuse.*

➤ *There must be balance in our leadership. They must choose to pursue wisdom from above and not necessarily stay bound by traditions and emotional attachment to the past.*

Chapter Two

The Origin of Haiti

*And hath made of one blood all nations of men
for to dwell on all the face of the earth,
and hath determined the times before appointed,
and the bounds of their habitation.* (Acts 17: 26)

Chapter Two

The Origin of Haiti

*T*he history always needs someone to beginning, for example in the beginning God created the heaven and the earth.

This allow you and I, to understand very clearly that God is the father of the history and as a father of history he always prepares those, he calls to continue the history now, that call is up to us whether rightly or wrongly we administered.

To aptly study the history of our own nation of Haiti, we must go back to the origin of mankind. The Bible tells us that Adam was the first man and Eve was the first woman and became Adam's wife. We are all descendants of Adam and Eve. God set them in the Garden of Eden and gave them a specific set of instructions so they could fulfill their purpose on the earth.

And the LORD God took the man, and put him into the garden of Eden to dress it and to keep it. And the LORD God commanded the man, saying, Of every tree of the garden thou mayest freely eat: But of the tree of the knowledge of good and evil, thou shalt not eat of it: for in the day that thou eatest thereof thou shalt surely die. (Genesis 2:15-17)

So God created man in his own image, in the image of God created he him; male and female created he them. And God blessed them, and God said unto them, Be fruitful, and multiply, and replenish the earth, and subdue it: and have dominion over the fish of the sea, and over the fowl of the air, and over every living thing that moveth upon the earth. (Genesis 1:27-28)

God blessed Adam and Eve saying be fruitful and multiply and replenish the earth. They were in perfect communion with God who gave them authority over all creation. But because of their disobedience, they lost their authority and we have inherited their sinful nature.

Wherefore, as by one man sin entered into the world, and death by sin; and so death passed upon all men, for that all have sinned. . . for all have sinned and come short of the glory of God. (Roman 5:12, 3:23)

But God, in His infinite love, prepared a plan of redemption through the second Adam.

> *For God so loved the world that he gave his only begotten son, that whosoever believeth in him should not perish but have everlasting life. For God sent not his son into the world to condemn the world; but that the world through him might be saved.* (John 3:16-17)

The authority that was lost because of man's sin of disobedience in the Garden of Eden was restored by the atoning sacrifice of the second Adam, who is Jesus Christ. He gave Himself as the redemption for our sins and died for us on the cross.

> *And for this cause he is the mediator of a new testament, that by mean of death, for the redemption of the transgressions that were under the first testament, they which are called might receive the promise of eternal inheritance.* (Hebrews 9:15)

> *Surely he hath borne our grief, and carried our sorrows: yet we did esteem him stricken, smitten of God, and afflicted. But he was wounded for our transgressions; he was bruised for our iniquities: the chastisement of our peace was upon Him; and with his stripes we are healed.* (Isaiah 53:4-5)

Since we inherited from the first Adam the sin that caused mankind's separation from God, we all need to realize our need to receive the benefit of the saving grace provided for us by the second Adam, Christ Jesus.

According to the eternal purpose which he pur-posed in Christ Jesus our Lord. In whom we have boldness and access with confidence by the faith of him. (Ephesians 3:11-12)

It is my honor to call on the name of the second Adam, who came being a king, he was born king, died as a king, resurrected king, king is back and will return king, and he will forever king, but he emptied himself, taking the form of a servant, becoming like human, Philippians 2: 7, he came to reconcile us with God, Jesus Christ, the son of the living God to help us understand where we have come from but also where we are going.

His name shall be called Wonderful, Counselor, the mighty God, the everlasting Father, and Prince of Peace. (Isaiah 9:6)

The Bible also sign grand men who chose to give up everything to serve his country with all their heart and marked the history positively. The island nation of Haiti has been a country that has made his-tory through the whole world for his courage, and his efforts as the first black republic to fight and take its independence, 1804. And many of us have the courage to recognize also that we have failed God from the beginning, of the founding of our nation.

There're many enormous marvels that are recorded in the Bible that has, marked the history of human beings: But I want to prove to you that God has never changed, he is still the same today tomorrow and forever.

The first was that in the beginning of universe human speak only one language, man joined to gather to rebel against God's plans. Wisely God confused the tongue of all human beings and from there all nations were formed in its own territory and its limits. *"Now, let us go down and there confuse their language so they will not understand the speech of his companion. So the LORD scattered them abroad from thence upon the face of the whole earth, and they stopped building the city. Genesis 11: 7.8 "_" when the high did inherit the nations, when he separated the sons of Adam, he set the bounds of the people. Deuteronomy 32:8.*

Second, as the whole world began moving forward, on the day of Pentecost those same people who speak only, one language and the beginning that God has changed their tongue for them not to be able to communicate to one another. On the, day of Pentecost the ones, that were found there under the power of the Holy Spirit, they spoke in the language of those, who was representing, his nation that day. "And they were all filled with the Holy Spirit and began to speak in other language as the Spirit gave them utterance. Acts 2: 4 ". Now I would like you to pay attention! Do not forget that the Bible has its own symbolic language and style you must see the facts and make the right conclusion, what was happening in the beginning of the Bible it is still repeating itself today. Because the king of Salome said there is nothing new under the sun.

The next marvel that God has done, in the eyes of the, whole world is to put all those tribe to gather that the French, took from the continent of Africa and bring them on the island nation of Haiti, Which means and the Indigenous language the high mountains land, God at that time saw the suffering of our fathers and unified all those tribes and made them to speak one, language to understand one another to be able to communicate and fight to be free from that slavery at the hand of the French. And, through that language we were able to be one and help other country. Today by the grace of God it called "Haitian".

And one man he made every nation of men for to dwell on all the face of the earth, and hath prefijad the order of time, and the limits of your room. Acts17:26.

This revelation is key, so that you know he already knew what would take place in the future what country would speak the language that was in his agenda. Haiti was already one of them.

The biggest mistake we made after almighty has brought us together to be one nation through that language called Haitian, as payment we betrayed Him, After showing his mercy in this very difficult time that our father was going through. Today I, ask God for forgiveness with, my entire Haitians fellow who accepted that we fall his love that he has for us the nation of Haiti.

Origin of the Haitian Nation

History shows us that each country has its origin and that its eventual growth was determined by the people who lived there and what outside influences infiltrated their culture and religion. We, the people of Haiti come from Africa. Our ancestors were brought here to Haiti as slaves.

There came a time in our history when we rebelled against slavery, but unfortunately we traded one form of slavery for another. On August 22, 1791, slaves in the northern region of the colony staged a revolt that began the <u>Haitian Revolution</u>. Tradition marks the beginning of the revolution at a <u>voodoo</u> ceremony at <u>Bois Caïman</u> (Alligator Woods) near Cap-Français. The call to arms was issued by a <u>Houngan</u> (voodoo priest) named <u>Dutty Boukman</u>. A vow made with pig's blood that our ancestors made with the devil at the ceremony of bois-caiman established the voodoo that is said to be the origin of all the disasters that have since come upon Haiti.

History tells us that this ceremony ultimately resulted in the liberation of the Haitian people from

> There came a time in our history when we rebelled against slavery, but unfortunately we traded one form of slavery for another.

59

French <u>colonial</u> rule in 1804, and the establishment of the first black people's <u>republic</u> in the history of the world-the second independent nation in the Americas. Haiti is the world's oldest black republic and one of the oldest republics in the <u>Western Hemisphere</u>. Had we but aligned ourselves with God instead of the devil our country would have grown and prospered.

The People Corrupted Themselves

Our people made the same mistakes that some of the people in the Bible did. When a culture or country chooses to worship idols instead of the one true God, they are breaking one of the commandments of God and will incur the consequences of their disobedience.

And it shall be, if thou do at all forget the LORD thy God, and walk after other gods, and serve them, and worship them, I testify against you this day that ye shall surely perish. As the nations which the LORD destroyeth before your face, so shall ye perish; because ye would not be obedient unto the voice of the LORD your God. (Deuteronomy 8:19-20)

"Forget not God's former dealings with thee." Here is the great secret of Divine Providence. Infinite wisdom and goodness are the source of all the changes and trials believers' experience. Israel had many bitter trials, but it was "to do them good."

"Would one suppose that such a people, after their slavery at the brick-kilns, should need the thorns of the wilderness to humble them? But such is man."[15]

The Israelites were tempted to seek help from the gods they learned about when they were in slavery in Egypt. When Moses was delayed on the Mountain of God, they asked Aaron to build them an idol that they could worship. They so angered God He told Moses He would destroy them all and start over with Moses.

And when the people saw that Moses delayed to come down out of the mount, the people gathered themselves together unto Aaron, and said unto him, Up, make us gods, which shall go before us; for as for this Moses, the man that brought us up out of the land of Egypt, we wot not what is become of him. (Exodus 32:1)

And the LORD said unto Moses, Go, get thee down; for thy people, which thou broughtest out of the land of Egypt, **have corrupted themselves: They have turned aside quickly out of the way which I commanded them:** *they have made them a molten calf, and have worshipped it, and have sacrificed thereunto, and said, These be thy gods, O Israel, which have brought thee up out of the land of Egypt. And the LORD said unto Moses,* **I have seen this people, and, behold, it is a stiff-necked people:** *Now therefore let me alone,* **that my wrath may wax hot against them, and that I may consume them: and I will make of thee a great nation.** (Exodus 32:7-10)

Notice that God told Moses that the people had corrupted themselves. Our people did the same thing when they turned to voodoo, reverting back to the "religion" of our African ancestry. *Vodou* is a <u>Haitian Creole</u> word that formerly referred to only to a small subset of Haitian rituals. It is descended from an <u>Ayizo</u> word referring to "mysterious forces or powers that govern the world and the lives of those who reside

> *They have corrupted themselves: They have turned aside quickly out of the way which I commanded them.*

within it, but also a range of artistic forms that function in conjunction with these *vodun* energies" (*Wikipedia*). In Haiti, practitioners occasionally use "vodou" to refer to Haitian religion generically, but it is more common for practitioners to refer to themselves as those who "serve the spirits" (*sèvitè*) by participating in ritual ceremonies, usually called a "service to the <u>lwa</u>" (*sèvis lwa*) or an "African service" (*sèvis gineh*). These terms can also be used to refer to the religion as a whole. Originally written as *vodun*, it is first recorded in *Doctrina Christiana*, a 1658 document written by the King of <u>Allada</u>'s ambassador to the court of <u>Philip IV of Spain</u> (Wikipedia).

As we study the history of our country we see that there were times of relative peace and prosperity. The Constitution of 1867 saw peaceful and progressive transitions in government that did much to improve the economy and stability of the Haitian nation and the condition of its people. The development of industrial sugar and rum industries near Port-au-Prince made Haiti, for a while, a model for economic growth in Latin American countries. However, this period of relative stability and prosperity was short lived and ended in 1911 when revolution broke out and the country slid once again into disorder and debt. From 1911 to 1915 there were six different Presidents, each of whom was killed or forced into exile. The revolutionary armies were formed by *cacos*, peasant brigands from the mountains of the north along the porous Dominican border, who were enlisted by rival political factions with promises of money to be paid after a successful revolution and an opportunity to plunder (*Wikipedia*). Our country was being destroyed from within.

A Kingdom Divided Cannot Stand

No country or people that fight against each other can stand. Jesus warned us of this very thing.

And if a kingdom be divided against itself, that kingdom cannot stand. And if a house be divided against itself, that house cannot stand. (Mark 3:24-25)

This internal struggle left our country open to the rise of a dictatorship. In February 1915, Vilbrun Guillaume Sam established a dictatorship, but in July, facing a new revolt, he massacred 167 political prisoners, all of whom were from elite families, and was lynched by a mob in Port-au-Prince. Shortly afterwards, responding to complaints to President Woodrow Wilson from American banks to which Haiti was deeply in debt, the United States occupied the country until 1930.

Our country appeared to be on an upward path when we finally had fully democratic elections in 1930, which were won by Sténio Vincent. The Garde was a new kind of military institution in Haiti. It was a force manned overwhelmingly by blacks, with a United States-trained black commander, Colonel Démosthènes

> And if a kingdom be divided against itself, that kingdom cannot stand. And if a house be divided against itself, that house cannot stand. (Mark 3:24-25).

Pétrus Calixte. The Garde was a national organization; it departed from the regionalism that had characterized most of Haiti's previous armies. In theory, its charge was apolitical—to maintain internal order, while supporting a popularly elected government. The Garde initially adhered to this role (*Wikipedia*). It appeared we were beginning to grow as a unified people.

However, President Vincent took advantage of the comparative national stability, which was being maintained by a professionalized military, to gain absolute power. A plebiscite permitted the transfer of all authority in economic matters from the legislature to the executive, but Vincent was not content with this expansion of his power. In 1935 he forced through the legislature a new constitution, which was also approved by plebiscite. The constitution praised Vincent, and it granted the executive sweeping powers to dissolve the legislature at will, to reorganize the judiciary, to appoint ten of twenty-one senators (and to recommend the remaining eleven to the lower house), and to rule by decree when the legislature was not in session. Although Vincent implemented some improvements in infrastructure and services, he brutally repressed his opposition, censored the press, and governed largely to benefit himself and a clique of merchants and corrupt military officers (*Wikipedia*).

Once again our nation faced an internal struggle for relief from "slavery." We still did not realize it was not a slavery that could be escaped from by civil war. The Revolution of 1946 was a novel development in Haiti's history, as the Garde assumed power as an institution, not as the instrument of a particular commander. The members of the junta, known as the Military Executive Committee (Comité Exécutif Militaire), were Garde commander Colonel Franck Lavaud, Major Antoine Levelt, and Major Paul E. Magloire, commander of the Presidential Guard. Upon taking power, the junta pledged to hold free elections. The junta also explored other options, but public clamor, which included public demonstrations in support of potential candidates, eventually forced the officers to make good on their promise (*Wikipedia*).

Once again our people were blinded from the truth and allowed a former Minister of Health who had earned a "reputation as a humanitarian" to establish another dictatorship. Duvalier's regime is regarded as one of the most repressive and corrupt of modern times, combining violence against political opponents with exploitation of <u>Vodou</u> to instill fear in the majority of the population. Duvalier's paramilitary police, officially the Volunteers for National Security but more commonly known as the <u>Tonton Macoutes</u> (named for a Vodou monster), carried out political murders, beatings, and intimidation. An estimated 30,000 Haitians were killed by his government. Incorporating many *houngans* into the ranks of the Macoutes, his public recognition of Vodou and its practitioners and his private adherence to Vodou ritual, combined with his reputed private knowledge of magic and sorcery, enhanced his popular persona among the common people and served as a peculiar form of legitimization (*Wikipedia*).

In the aftermath of the Duvalier dictatorship, a number of individuals, including many houngan, sought to organize means of defense for Haitian Vodou. One of the first leading houngan to formally organize other houngan in solidarity was <u>Wesner Morency</u> (1959–2007), who established the Vodou Church of Haiti in 1998 (registered in 2001 by the Ministry of Justice) and the Commission Nationale pour la Structuration de Vodou (CONAVO). Another individual who has pursued the organization of houngan is <u>Max Beauvoir</u>, who established and heads the <u>National Confederation of Haitian Vodou</u>.[16]

Jehovah God, in His mercy had given us this land, just as He had given Canaan to the Jewish people. Haiti, the name of our country, means in the Indian language: high land, mountainous land. But through our ignorance, we have turned away from God to serve Satan, the devil, and his hangmen.

> **Through our ignorance, we have turned away from God to serve Satan, the devil and his hangmen.**

Haiti in Service to Satan

Our nation has for many years held onto a negative practice that has not been pleasing to God. Voodoo comes as an inheritance from our forefathers. They bequeathed it to us and we have accepted into our culture as if there is no other choice available to us. Voodoo is a satanic religion that became an "official religion" in Haiti as of April 8, 2003 (BBC news). For over two centuries our government has been under the dominion of the satanic regime. Our leaders have been under the influence of darkness which, in the eyes of God, is an abomination.

He made his son pass through the fire, and observed times, and used enchantments, and dealt with familiar spirits and wizards: he wrought much wickedness in the sight of the Lord, to provoke Him to anger. (2 Kings 21:6)

The king of Manasseh, when he was ruling his country, provoked God by reinstating pagan worship and reversed the real principal commandment that was established by Jehovah God Almighty for the nation of Israel after they came out from Egypt. He made the religion of witchcraft official and encouraged his people to communicate with all types of spirits. King Manasseh gave no thought to these actions. Instead of bringing God's blessings to his people, he forced them to be cursed.

The time eventually came for Manasseh to pay for his actions. God used the king of the Syrians as an example and deported him to Babylonia in the year 650 B.C., far away from his own people, as punishment for his abominations in the presence of God. The almighty God does not sit back and do nothing and allow you to escape the consequences of your sin.

Our generation has the privilege to see how our God has dealt with President Jean Bentrand Aristide twice in Haitian history, just like he did with Manasseh. The first time was in 1991 after he was elected by the Haitian people. Aristide was planning to renew the pact that our ancestors made with the devil for 200 years, which was ending in 1991. However, God and His magnificent compassion and the love He has for His people didn't let that happen even though the country was still dedicated to Satan. God used President George

W. Bush and senior general Raoul Cedras, the head of the Haitian army, to deport Aristide from Haiti. God showed humanity that His mighty glory goes far behind our understandings. The second time was after Aristide made voodoo the official religion in Haiti on April 8, 2003. Again, God utilized President George W. Bush in 2004 to deport Aristide to Africa for doing the devil's will.

God taught Aristide a lesson just like He did to the King of Manasseh — that He rules everything in heaven and on earth and that He will use whoever He needs to accomplish His purpose. Manasseh repented of his actions and in his affliction, realized that God is not a toy to play with. God allowed Manasseh to return back to Israel to prove himself, just as He allowed Aristide to return, but no one knows if Aristide repented and returned back to God when he returned to Haiti Friday the 18th of March 2011.

Your president will pay for his actions as he serves as the head of the nation and the nation will pay the consequences as well. Remember, the universe belongs to God and He will hold every man accountable who crosses the line — think before you cross it. Did God change? No. He is the same God and will not change His position for anyone.

I have a lot of respect for everyone, especially those that have made it to official positions, but the fact is that I am dealing with you according to the truth of the living God. The Bible says, "The Lord spake to Manasseh and to his people, but they would not harken, wherefore the Lord brought upon them the captains of the host of the king of Assyria, which took Manasseh among the thorns and bound him with feters and carried him to Babylon" (2 Chronicles 33:10).

The Prophet Isaiah sent forth many warnings about committing such abominations against the Lord. We would be wise to heed these warnings!

I have spread out My hands all the day long to a rebellious people, who walk in a way that is not good, after their own thoughts—A people who provoke Me to My face continually, sacrificing [to idols] in gardens and burning incense upon bricks [instead of at God's prescribed altar]; Who sit among the graves [trying to talk with the dead] and lodge among the secret places [or caves where familiar spirits were thought to dwell]; who eat swine's flesh, and the broth of abominable and loathsome things is in their vessels; (Isaiah 65:2-4 AMP)

A Trumpet Is Blown

Shall a trumpet be blown in the city, and the people not are afraid? Shall there be evil in a city,

*and the Lord hath not done it? Surely the Lord
God will do nothing, but he revealed his secret
unto his servants the prophets.* (Amos 3:6-7)

There are numerous protests among our people
that the cyclones and earthquakes our country has
experienced are merely natural phenomena. Though
that is true, nothing can happen in the sky, the universe or on the earth without God's will. Jesus proved
that the wind and seas obey Him in Matthew 8:27.
We also read of the plagues God brought against the
Egyptians who chose to enslave God's people and
do evil in His sight. After many warnings from God,
our people still refused to turn away from the evil.
On January 12, 2010, at 4:55 p.m. according to my
watch, the most horrible earthquake in the history of
Haiti struck our land. Many began to cry out and ask
why did this happen to our beautiful country and to
seek rescue from the one true God.

*They that see thee shall narrowly look upon thee,
and consider thee, saying, is this man that made
the earth to tremble, that did shake kingdoms.*
(Isaiah 14:16)

After much analysis, I came to the conclusion
that God expects us to continue to call upon Him to
fix our problems in Haiti just like we did on January
12, 2010. God wants all Haitians to be united and
repent with all our hearts, but not because of the
earthquake. Rather God wants us to come to Him

because our conscience trembles and we are pushed to remorse from our iniquities.

Stand in awe, and sin not: commune with your own heart upon your bed, and be still. (Psalms 4:4)

Let us draw near with a true heart in full assurance of faith, having our hearts sprinkled from an evil conscience and our bodies washed with pure water. (Hebrews 10:2)

God does not want us to call on Him only because of the repercussions we have suffered from the earthquake, but because of an awareness of our spiritual state. He would have us awaken and move away from the evil ways that our ancestors followed and that many of our people still continue to follow today.

But now in Christ Jesus ye who sometimes were far off are made nigh by the blood of Christ. (Ephesians 2:13)

He that covereth his sins shall not prosper: but whoso confesseth and foresaketh them shall have mercy. (Proverbs 28:13)

What happened should show us that we must put our faith in God not in the evil worship of our ancestors. I had the privilege to speak to an African brother after the earthquake of January 12, 2010, at the international airport of Puerto Rico. He said he was deeply touched by what happened in Haiti. I told him that God's hand is upon us and it was surely time for revival in Haiti. I asked him for information about the spread of the gospel in Africa. He replied that there is much progress there and that on the days of worship, churches are full to bursting. If many of our African brothers have rejected the practice of voodoo, why don't we follow their examples?

God has allowed me to also talk with a well-known Haitian senator about the spiritual problem of our country, which he immediately understood and accepted. The majority of the population practice voodoo and the rest are atheist. The fact that I was born into a Christian family, did not make me automatically a Christian. I thank the Lord that He protected me from the satanic influence I was exposed to in Haiti. I was on the road to hell with Satan, the enemy of Haiti. It was in the United States of America that I finally returned to God through our Lord and Savior Jesus Christ, and therefore I made a firm decision to follow through and help my people and my nation turn their hearts and minds to God as well.

Our heavenly Father is waiting for each of His children to turn away from evil and return to His arms of love.

But now in Christ Jesus ye who sometimes were far off are made nigh by the blood of Christ. (Ephesians 2:13)

What have we learned about the Origin of the Haitian Nation?

➢ *Our ancestors were brought here from Africa as slaves.*

➢ *We rebelled but unfortunately we traded one form of slavery for another.*

➢ *Our people made the same mistakes that some of the people in the Bible did.*

➢ *A kingdom divided against itself cannot stand.*

➢ *Our people corrupted themselves and made a deal with the devil.*

➢ *A vow made with pig's blood is the origin of all the disasters that have come upon Haiti.*

➢ *Through our ignorance, we have turned away from God to serve Satan.*

➢ *For over two centuries Haiti has been in the Service of Satan.*

But now in Christ Jesus ye who sometimes were far off are made nigh by the blood of Christ. (Ephesians 2:13)

Chapter Three

Similarities Between Israel and Haiti

*He received them at their hand, and fashioned it
with a graving tool,
after he had made it a molten calf;
and they said, these be thy gods,
O Israel, which brought thee up out of the land of
Egypt.*
(Exodus 32:4)

Chapter Three

Similarities Between Israel and Haiti

I made a deep study on Haiti and have concluded
that the history of Israel and Haiti are very similar. The people of Israel have played a very important role in world history in the social, material, and
spiritual aspects of life. Israel experienced slavery
that resulted from ingratitude and disobedience to
God's Word. God even warned Abraham that this
would happen to them when they turned their backs
on Him and did evil in His sight.

> *And he said unto Abram, know of a surety that*
> *thy seed shall be a stranger in a land that is not*
> *theirs, and shall serve them; and they shall afflict*
> *them four hundred years.* (Genesis 15:13)

Ingratitude to God

God's prophecy to Abraham came true and after four hundred and thirty years in slavery in Egypt, God sent a deliverer to lead His people to their Promised Land (Exodus 12:40-51). God sent Moses to the children of Israel to lead them to Canaan. After these people experienced all the wonders of God as He brought them out from under Pharaoh and led them with a cloud by day and a pillar of fire by night, the Israelites repaid God with ingratitude. When they reached the banks of the Red Sea and saw that Pharaoh and his army were pursuing them, the ungrateful children of Israel cried out to the Lord and complained.

And they said unto Moses, Because there were no graves in Egypt, hast thou taken us away to die in the wilderness? Wherefore hast thou dealt thus with us, to carry us forth out of Egypt? Is not this the word that we did tell thee in Egypt, saying, Let us alone, that we may serve the Egyptians? For it had been better for us to serve the Egyptians, than that we should die in the wilderness. (Exodus 14:11-12)

> **Israel experienced slavery that resulted from ingratitude and disobedience to God's Word.**

Even after they witnessed the parting of the Red Sea, when the people became tired, thirsty and hungry after less than two months in the wilderness, they once again showed ingratitude to the God of their deliverance.

> *And the whole congregation of the children of Israel murmured against Moses and Aaron in the wilderness: And the children of Israel said unto them, Would to God we had died by the hand of the LORD in the land of Egypt, when we sat by the flesh pots, and when we did eat bread to the full; for ye have brought us forth into this wilderness, to kill this whole assembly with hunger.* (Exodus 16:2-3)

The provisions brought from Egypt were spent by the middle of the second month and they murmured. It is no new thing for the greatest kindness to be basely represented as the greatest injuries. They so far undervalued their deliverance that they wished they had died in Egypt. We cannot suppose they had plenty in Egypt, nor could they fear dying for want in the wilderness, while they had flocks and herds: none talk more absurdly than murmurers. When we begin to fret, we ought to consider, that God hears all our murmurings. God promises a speedy and constant supply. He tried whether they would trust him and serve him, and it appeared how ungrateful they were. When God plagued the Egyptians, it was to make them know he was their Lord; when he provided for the Israelites, it was to make them know he was their God.[17]

How unreasonable and absurd the charge against Moses and Aaron! How ungrateful and impious against God! After all their experiences of the divine wisdom, goodness, and power, we pause and wonder over the sacred narrative of their hardness and unbelief. But the expression of feeling is contagious in so vast a multitude.[18]

Ingratitude Turns to Disobedience

While Moses was seeking spiritual provisions for them on Mount Sinai, the Israelites were allowing their impatience and ingratitude to grow into blatant disobedience to God. When he descended and found that they had made for themselves an idol to worship and even gave it credit for their deliverance from Egypt, he was angry and shocked after all God had done for the people of Israel.

> *And all the people brake off the golden earrings which were in their ears, and brought them unto Aaron. And he received them at their hand, and fashioned it with a graving tool, after he had made it a molten calf: and **they said, These be thy gods, O Israel, which brought thee up out of the land of Egypt.** And when Aaron saw it, he built an altar before it; and Aaron made proclamation, and said, Tomorrow is a feast to the LORD. And they rose up early on the morrow, and offered burnt offerings, and brought peace*

offerings; and the people sat down to eat and to drink, and rose up to play. (Exodus 32:3-6)

Aaron produced the shape of an ox or calf, giving it some finish with a graving tool. They offered sacrifice to this idol. Having set up an image before them, and so changed the truth of God into a lie, their sacrifices were abomination. Had they not, only a few days before, in this very place, heard the voice of the Lord God speaking to them out of the midst of the fire, Thou shalt not make to thyself any graven image? Had they not themselves solemnly entered into covenant with God, that they would do all he had said to them, and would be obedient? (Exodus 24:7).[19]

Currently the same acts occur within our nation. The Haitian people are acting with the same spirit of ingratitude as the people of Israel did by saying we have our independence through voodoo. The people of Israel made a golden calf with their own hands and put their confidence in the golden calf. Our ancestors sacrificed a pig and have proclaimed that it was the pig that helped us obtain the victory of independence. Could a golden calf have delivered the children of Israel from Egypt? Could a pig have helped our people win our liberation from slavery? It was impossible for Israel to deliver themselves from slavery just as Haiti could not have won their liberation without the intervention of God's masterly plan. The devil does not release people from bondage, he holds them in bondage. By our ancestors entering into a union with the devil, however, they set our country up to receive the consequences of disobedience just as the Israelites did.

Our land is sick because we make it sick through our abomination that we continues to do.

There are three types of sin. The fist sin is the original sin that we all inherited from Adam and eve, injected in our blood by the spiritual DNA, from the garden. "wherefore, as by one man sin entered into the world. . . Rom 5:12" The second sin is the individual sin that everyone has free; you must narrow it down in the name of Jesus or embraced it by your own will. "The soul that sinned, it shall die. Ezekiel 18:4" The third sin is a collective sin that we all agreed to commit abomination against the nature of God. "For all have sinned, and come short of the glory of God. Rom.3:23". As a Haitian, I am commanding all Haitian's to wake up from the deep darkness that causes them to sleep the darkness that has caused us to sleep for more than two hundred years, we must repent from that sin that we all agreed in 1791/14 of august, when we did such a wicked vow with devil for our independence when God did already give us the independence before the whole world foundation. *"And hath made of one blood all nations of men for to dwell on all the face of the earth, and hath determined the times before appointed, and the bounds of their habitation. Acts 17: 26"*

We have done the same we have agreed to make that vow with the devil, we have done the same no doubt that today we all need to agree together to say no to the vow and that big sin that we committed against the sovereignty of God that hinders the prosperity of our nation. We don't have any other hope if we don't return to God and give the country to God "And the children of Israel said unto the Lord, We have sinned do thou unto us whatsoever seemed good unto thee; deliver us only; we pray thee, this day. And they put away the strange gods from among them, and served the Lord and his soul was grieved for the misery of Israel. Judges 10:15-16".

History shows, a lot of great men who did a lot of thing, some of them they almost conquered the whole world, pharaoh, the great Alexander, Jules Cesar, Christophe Colombo, Napoleon Bonaparte, Adolph Hitler, Dessalines Jean Jacques and some other. I don't care who you are, let me talk to you very clear with the authority of Jesus Christ, if you don't repent from your wicked sins, without a doubt no matter who you are president, senator, deputy, mayor, judge, lawyer; whatever religion you are, If you don't turn away from your wicked sin, the gate of hell is wide open waiting for you. I advise you to return to God so you can save your soul through the blood of Jesus Christ.

After all have you done in this present world, if God made the way for you before the world foundation through the blood of his son Jesus Christ, you work for nothing "For what shall it profit a man, if he shall gain the whole world, and lose his own soul? Marc 8:36";" Father, I will that they also, whom thou hast given me, be with me where I am; that they may behold my Glory, which thou hast given me: for thou lovedst me before the foundation of the world. John 17:24"

The early lapse into idolatry was always mentioned as an aggravation of the Israelites) subsequent apostasies.[20] I fear the same can be said of Haiti.

And the LORD said unto Moses, Whosoever hath sinned against me, him will I blot out of my book. Therefore now go, lead the people unto the place of which I have spoken unto thee: behold, mine Angel shall go before thee: nevertheless in the day when I visit I will visit their sin upon them. And the LORD plagued the people, because they made the calf, which Aaron made. (Exodus 32:33-35)

The Consequence of Disobedience to God

Behold, I set before you this day a blessing and a curse; A blessing, if ye obey the commandments of the LORD your God, which I command you this day: And a curse, if ye will not obey the commandments of the LORD your God, but turn aside out of the way which I command you this day, to go after other gods, which ye have not known. (Deuteronomy 11:26-28)

The Haitian people are acting with the same spirit of ingratitude as the people of Israel did by saying we have our independence through voodoo.

As the Israelites were preparing to cross over into the Promised Land, Moses sums up all the arguments for obedience in two words, the blessing and the curse. He charged the people to choose which way they would go. Obedience and disobedience is a choice.

The Psalms also record the accounts of what the children of Israel did in the wilderness so we can learn from their mistakes and not fall into disobedience and rebellion as they did and provoke God's anger.

> *He wrought wonders before their fathers In the land of Egypt, in the field of Zoan. He divided the sea and caused them to pass through, And He made the waters stand up like a heap. Then He led them with the cloud by day And all the night with a light of fire. He split the rocks in the wilderness And gave them abundant drink like the ocean depths. He brought forth streams also from the rock And caused waters to run down like rivers. Yet they still continued to sin against Him, To rebel against the Most High in the desert.* (Psalm 78:12-17 NAS)

The Bible teaches us that disobedience is one of the greatest forms of rebellion. Nehemiah recorded the pattern the Israelites followed of disobedience and rebellion against God and how because of it He allowed their enemies to oppress them.

Nevertheless they were disobedient, and rebelled against thee, and cast thy law behind their backs, and slew thy prophets which testified against them to turn them to thee, and they wrought great provocations. Therefore thou deliveredst them into the hand of their enemies, who vexed them: and in the time of their trouble, when they cried unto thee, thou heardest them from heaven; and according to thy manifold mercies thou gavest them saviours, who saved them out of the hand of their enemies. (Nehemiah 9:26-27)

Is not their conduct a specimen of human nature? Let us study the history of our land, and our own history. Let us recollect our advantages from childhood, and ask what were our first returns? Let us frequently do so that we may be kept humble, thankful, and watchful. Let us all remember that pride and obstinacy are sins which ruin the soul. But it is often as hard to persuade the broken-hearted to hope, as formerly it was to bring them to fear. Behold this sweet promise, a God ready to pardon! Instead of keeping away from God under a sense of unworthiness, let us come boldly to the throne of grace, that we may obtain mercy, and find grace to help in time of need. He is a God ready to pardon.[21] Oh, that the people of Haiti would learn from the stories of the Israelites and call out to the God of their salvation!

Disobedience leads inevitably to punishment, and punishment undoubtedly produces all kinds of trouble and tribulation such as earthquakes, pestilence, and the like. God has given us examples of the consequences of disobedience all throughout the Bible. Saul was the first king who ruled the people of Israel. After his government had been established, he disobeyed God by making a decision without consulting Him. Because of this, "there was a famine in the days of David three years, year after year; and David inquired of the Lord. And the Lord answered, it is for Saul and for his bloody house, because he slew the Gibeonites" (2 Samuel 21:1).

David also erred by disobeying God during his reign as King. Look at what the second king of Israel brought upon his people by being disobedience.

I have sinned greatly in that I have done: and now, I beseech thee, O Lord, take away the iniquity of thy servant, for I have done very foolishly. For when David arose in the morning, the word of the Lord came unto the prophet Gad, David's seer, saying, go and say unto David, thus saith the Lord, I offer thee three things; choose thee one of them, that I may do it unto thee. So Gad came to David, and told him, and said unto him, shall seven years of famine come unto thee in thy land? Or wilt thou flee three months before thine enemies in your land, or flee three months before thine enemies, while they pursue thee? Or that there be three days' pestilence in thy land? Now advise, and see what answer in shall return to him that sent me. And David said unto Gad: I am in a great strait: let us fall now into the hands of the Lord; for his mercies are great: and let me not fall into the hands of man.

So the Lord sent a pestilence upon Israel from the morning even to the time appointed: and there died of the people from Dan to Beersheba, Seventy thousand men. And when the angel stretched out his hand upon Jerusalem to destroy it, the Lord repented him of the evil, and said to the angel that destroyed the people, it is enough: Stay now thine hand. And the angel of the Lord was by the threshing place of Araunah the Jebusites. And David spoke unto the lord when he saw the angel that smote the people, and said, Lo, I have sinned! And I have done wickedly: but these sheep, what have they done? Let thine hand, I pray thee, be against me and my father's house! (2 Samuel 24:10-17)

> **Haiti has been under the punishment of God for more than two centuries because of that disobedience.**

What seem to be simple to you is perceived differently in the eyes of God especially if it does not reflect His will. We see the similarities between what we read about Israel and what is happening now in Haiti. Our ancestors were no better than King Saul and King David. Just as these kings disobeyed God, our ancestors also disobeyed God when they made the vow with Satan instead of turning to the Lord for our country's independence. Haiti has been under the punishment of God for more than two centuries because of that disobedience. We can see with our own eyes the same pattern of punishment in our land and on the Haitian people. When it's not a cyclone which causes frequent flooding, it is earthquake after which we begin to turn our hearts back to God in hopes of attaining relief. But then like the children of Israel, we forget it is God who is to be our source and we bring yet another punishment upon ourselves.

The question that I would ask is who is the author of all these disasters? Again we can study the Bible to see how the Israelites brought these disasters on themselves and compare their behavior and the consequences of their disobedience to the conditions in our own country.

> *And the LORD spake unto Moses and unto Aaron, saying, How long shall I bear with this evil congregation, which murmur against me? I have heard the murmurings of the children of Israel, which they murmur against me.*

> *Say unto them,* **As truly as I live, saith the LORD, as ye have spoken in mine ears, so will I do to you:** *Your carcases shall fall in this wilderness; and all that were numbered of you, according to your whole number, from twenty years old and upward, which have murmured against me, doubtless ye shall not come into the land, concerning which I sware to make you dwell therein, save Caleb the son of Jephunneh, and Joshua the son of Nun. But your little ones, which ye said*

should be a prey, them will I bring in, and they shall know the land which ye have despised.

But as for you, your carcases, they shall fall in this wilderness. And your children shall wander in the wilderness forty years, and bear your whoredoms, until your carcases be wasted in the wilderness. **After the number of the days in which ye searched the land, even forty days, each day for a year, shall ye bear your iniquities, even forty years, and ye shall know my breach of promise.** *I the LORD have said,* **I will surely do it unto all this evil congregation, that are gathered together against me: in this wilderness they shall be consumed, and there they shall die.** (Numbers 14:26-35)

The people brought these punishments upon themselves. The very words they spoke became the punishment they received. They had turned their hearts away from God even though He had given them opportunities to turn away from trusting in idols.

Our ancestors turned their hearts to Satan instead of God when they sought independence from their oppressors. God used their own words and actions as a way to punish them just like He did to the people of Israel. Our ancestors turned to Satan so God has used Satan, the author of the disobedience, to punish us for our disobedience like He did the Israelites.

And the Lord said who shall entice Ahab king of Israel, that he may go up and fall at Ramoth-Gilead? And one spake saying after this manner and another saying after that manner. Then there came out a spirit, and stood before the Lord, and said, I will entice him. And the Lord said unto him, wherewith? And he said, I will go out, and be a lying spirit in the mouth of all his prophets. And the Lord said thou shalt entice him, and thou shalt also prevail: go out and do even so. (2 Chronicles 18:19-21)

Why have our leaders not seen the truth and done what is needed to halt the punishment that has raged down upon us? It is because they hold onto the false belief that we gained our independence from voodoo. Satan played a dirty trick to our ancestors and because of their choices, all these types of punishments have been handed down to their children. God has given us opportunities as He did the children of Israel to stop the flow of disobedience and turn our hearts and minds back to God, the true source of our provision and protection.

When King David was convicted of the sin of King Saul and saw the suffering of his people, he repented and sought how to reverse the curse by doing what was right in the eyes of the Lord. It is the same with the prophet Jonah. First he ran away from what the Lord had called him to do to help save the people of Ninevah. Then when he saw that the boat he was trying to escape in was going to sink, he had the courage to say that it was his sin that caused the trouble.

> *Then said they unto him, what shall we do unto thee, that the sea may be calm unto us? For the sea wrought, and was tempestuous. And he said unto them, Take me up, and cast me forth into the sea so shall the sea be calm unto you: For I know that for my sake is great tempest is upon you. So they took up Jonah and cast him forth into the sea and the sea ceased from her raging. Then the men feared the Lord exceedingly, and offered a sacrifice.* (Jonah 1:11-12, 15-16)

Instead of our leaders repenting for the wickedness of our ancestors and the leaders after them, they afflict the people with more pain. God will not leave it that way because all the prayers of the faithful servants, who tirelessly implore God for Haiti. God is faithful to His word and will heed the prayers of the righteous.

> *For the eyes of the Lord are over the righteous, and his ears are open unto their prayers, but the face of the Lord is against them that do evil.* (1 Peter 3:12)

> *So shall my word be that goeth forth out of my mouth: it shall not return unto me void, but it shall accomplish that which I please, and it shall prosper in the thing whereto I sent it.* (Isaiah 55:11)

The Truth Will Set Us Free

Now the word of the LORD came unto Jonah the son of Amittai, saying, Arise, go to Nineveh, that great city, and cry against it; for their wickedness is come up before me. (Jonah 1:1-2)

Instead of our leaders repenting for the wickedness of our ancestors and the leaders after them, they afflict the people with more pain.

Just as God sent Jonah to the people of Ninevah, He will send those who will bring the truth to the people of Haiti. Even though Jonah had to be convinced through his own experiences to obey the Lord and go to the people of Ninevah, the king of Ninevah and his nobles believed the message was from God and heeded the warnings. God saw their true repentance and did not send the punishment upon them.

*So **the people of Nineveh believed God**, and proclaimed a fast, and put on sackcloth, from the greatest of them even to the least of them. For word came unto the king of Nineveh, and he arose from his throne, and he laid his robe from him, and covered him with sackcloth, and sat in ashes. And he caused it to be proclaimed and published through Nineveh **by the decree of the king and his nobles**, saying, Let neither man nor beast, herd nor flock, taste any thing: let them not feed,* *nor drink water: But let man and beast be covered with sackcloth, and cry mightily unto God: yea,* **let them turn every one from his evil way, and from the violence that is in their hands.** *Who can tell if God will turn and repent, and turn away from his fierce anger, that we perish not?* **And God saw their works, that they turned from their evil way; and God repented of the evil, that he had said that he would do unto them; and he did it not.** (Jonah 3:5-10)

Currently, there are those among our people who argue that we got our independence through God's intervention, but there are still others who argue that we received it from the voodoo. Knowing the truth that comes from Jesus is the only thing that will give true liberation to man, now and into eternity.

Jesus saith unto him, I am the way, the truth, and the life: no man cometh unto the Father, but by me. (John 14:6)

So Jesus said to those Jews who had believed in Him, If you abide in My word [hold fast to My teachings and live in accordance with them], you are truly My disciples. And you will know the Truth, and the Truth will set you free. (John 8:31-32 AMP)

The Spirit of the Lord God is upon me; because the Lord has anointed me to preach good tidings unto the meek; he hath sent me to bind up the brokenhearted, to proclaim liberty to the captives, and the opening of the prisoner to them that are bound. (Isaiah 61:1)

God has allowed the Haitian people to suffer only to capture their attention. God is waiting to bring us life and life more abundantly through Jesus, His Son. What He needs is that we repentant of evil and humble ourselves before Him. When the leaders and the people of Ninevah believed God and turned their hearts from evil, God saw and withdrew His punishments. If we take this knowledge from God's Word and truly learn from the past, we too can come to God and be truly set free from bondage and move into the abundant life He so wants to give us.

I have sworn by myself, the word is gone out of my mouth in righteousness, and shall not return, that unto me every knee shall bow, every tongue shall swear. (Isaiah 45:23)

Blotting out the handwriting of ordinances that was against us, which was contrary to us, and took it out of the way, nailing in to cross. (Colossians 2:14)

Jesus explained it very clearly, "The thief cometh not, but for to steal, and to kill, and to destroy: I am come that they might have life, and that they might have it more abundantly" (John 10:10).

What have we learned from our comparison of Israel and Haiti?

➤ *Israel experienced slavery that resulted from ingratitude and disobedience to God's Word.*

➤ *The Haitian people are acting with the same spirit of ingratitude as the people of Israel did by saying we have our independence through voodoo.*

➤ *The people of Israel made a golden calf with their own hands and put their confidence in the golden calf.*

➤ *Our ancestors sacrificed a pig and have proclaimed that this was the pig that helped us obtain the victory of independence*

➤ *Just as King Saul and King David disobeyed God, our ancestors also disobeyed God when they made the vow with Satan instead of turning to the Lord for our country's independence.*

➤ *Haiti has been under the punishment of God for more than two centuries because of that disobedience.*

➤ *Like the children of Israel, we forget it is God who is to be our source and we bring yet another punishment upon ourselves.*

➤ *Like the king of Ninevah, his nobles and the people believed the message was from God and heeded the warnings, we too must heed this warning.*

➤ *Then God will see our true repentance and not send further punishments upon our beloved Haiti.*

Chapter Four

Haiti! Return to God

If my people, which are called by my name, shall humble themselves, and pray, and seek my face, and turn from their wicked ways; then will I hear from heaven, and will forgive their sin and will heal their land. (2 Chronicles 7:14)

Chapter Four

Haiti! Return to God

*H*aiti has more than two hundred years of independence, more than two hundred years out from under the grace of God, and more than two hundred years of disobedience from the will of God. This is why everything is happening in our country. The problems of Haiti are neither material nor social. The problems of Haiti will not be solved by supplying food or material assistance only because it is written, "Man shall not live by bread alone, but by every word that proceeded out of the mouth of God" (Matthew 4:4).

On several occasions I have heard people say that Haiti is the poorest country in the western hemisphere. There is more to the "poverty" in Haiti then is expressed by the pictures sent around the world by the media. In fact, when a country turns away from God, it is more than impoverished. Our people have accepted a poverty mentality.

In 2006 I returned to Haiti with an American missionary pastor. I took him to visit places all around our country and he was very surprised at what he saw. When I asked him why he was surprised, he said he was attracted to the beauty of our mountains. He saw that Haiti is a beautiful place. What he was seeing was in deep contrast to the perception he had formed in his mind from pictures of poverty shown on television that were being used to extort money. What he had seen and heard about Haiti was not the whole truth.

What Is the TruthS

Haiti is composed of ten geographical departments with Port au Prince as the capital. Haiti is a country rich materially and socially. I have traveled extensively around the country and I see the grace that God has given to this nation. In Haiti we have a diversity of resources, including human resources, a third of Haiti's population is under 15 years and 60% of the population is under 25 years, Haiti is a tropical country, has incalculable natural resources and undeveloped as wind, solar, natural beaches, attractions unlike anything found elsewhere and mining immeasurable, argentiferous gold deposits are in Morne grand bois, Morne Bossa, in la Faille in Douvray and Blondin, Vallieres, and in Meme Casséus. Bauxite is found in Miragoane, in savane bourrique in goyavier (St. Marc) etc. . . mention other natural resources that are the envyof many, including oil and uranium, For more information, visit the located of the Bureau of Mines in Haiti or following that link: http://bme. gouv.ht/carriere/carriere3/index.html

Shortly after the terrible earthquake in Haiti, gold mining companies located another area of gold and trou Du nord that was worth 20 billion in U.S. dollars. (nbcnews.com) The question is, what are they going to do for the 10 million people that live in Haiti and the 4 million Haitian people that live around the world, not to mention the one million people that haven't had a place to stay since the earthquake. We need to realize that Haiti is the poorest country on the Latin American continent. After the earthquake a lot of countries around the world took the opportunity to quickly intervene and take advantage of the earthquake situation to pretend that they were helping Haiti, while at the same time, they were taking care of business. The fact is that some of the countries were making a fortune in the name of Haiti.

I believe the entire world is watching what is happening in Haiti and waiting to see what they are going to do with the nation they have been calling poor. When the earthquake hit on the 12th of January in 2010, billions of dollars were raised by powerful politicians, authors, actors, artists, and people broken hearted by the devastation in Haiti, the question is, where did all the money go that those people gave to help Haiti recover? More than one million Haitian people are still in the streets after the earthquake, the youth don't have a new system of education yet and there isn't a new development project for the people to work. The fact is, they are making themselves rich from the wealth of Haiti. The corrupt groups of Haiti are selling the country off little by little because they hate to see the nation of Haiti move forward. Three firms are considering mining in Haiti, but so far only SOMINE has full concession to take metals out of the mountains. Those permits are for 31 square miles and were negotiated in 1996 under President Rene Preval and require the firm to hire Haitians whenever possible.

We are poor because we accept the poverty that has been spoken over us. Though we made need financial and material aid from other countries, what we really need are those who will teach us the principles needed for us to grow and prosper on our own. When someone really cares about a country like Haiti, they will not just keep sending us food; they will teach us how to produce our own food.

"You can give a hungry man a fish, but tomorrow you will have to give him another fish and another the next day and the day after that and so on. But if you teach a man how to fish, he will be able to catch his own fish and feed himself and his family as well."

On another occasion I met an American investor in Miami. While we were enjoying dinner together, he told me he had just returned from Haiti and said he was jealous of my country. I asked him what he meant by that and he said that he was deeply affected by the trop-

> **When a country turns away from God, it is more than impoverished. Our people have accepted a poverty mentality.**

ical climate of the country. He called it a natural paradise.

These people had never seen or heard the truth about Haiti. Many of our own people believe the lie that we are an impoverished nation with no hope for growth or prosperity. It is time we stop believing the lie. Because our people have chosen to partner with Satan, they believe his lies. We must remember that Satan is the father of lies and he is a thief that is out to steal all that we have. He wants to steal our hearts and fill our minds with his lies. He wants to kill our families and steal our future generations. He wants to destroy our land and steal our prosperity. Jesus said, "The thief cometh not, but for to steal, and to kill, and to destroy: I am come that they might have life, and that they might have it more abundantly" (John 10:10).

The solution is to drive people towards the path of truth. Jesus said, "I am the way, the truth, and the life" (John 14:6). Jesus also said, "If you abide in My word [hold fast to My teachings and live in accordance with them], you are truly My disciples. And you will know the Truth, and the Truth will set you free" (John 8:31-32 AMP). Jesus came to bring us life and life more abundantly. How much clearer can it be said?

The truth is that the Haitian people have to repent of all sins and evil deeds that our ancestors had committed before the face of God and that we continue to practice even today. We have to tell Satan he is a liar and we will no longer allow him access to our minds, our families, and our land.

If my people, which are called by my name, shall humble themselves, and pray, and seek my face, and turn from their wicked ways; then will I hear from heaven, and will forgive their sin and will heal their land. (2 Chronicles 7:14)

Haiti, Wake Up!

And the times of this ignorance God winked at; but now commandeth all men everywhere to repent. (Acts 17:30)

Haiti, it is time to wake up from this spiritual sleep. It is way passed the time to wake up from this sleep you've been immersed in for over two hundred years.

Awake thou that sleepest, and arises from the dead and Christ shall give thee light. (Ephesians 5:14)

Jesus said, "I am the light of the world: he that followeth me shall not walk in darkness, but shall have the light of life" (John 8:12). Submit yourself entirely to

> **I suggest it is time for us to turn to the Creator of heaven and earth; individually and a nation.**

God through Christ and you will not be disappointed.

We have been fumbling around in the dark too long. It is time to come out into the light of Jesus

104

Christ because He is the light. We have gone for help to all sorts of people and all kinds of spirits but we were just led further into darkness and deceived by all of them. I suggest it is time for us to turn to the Creator of heaven and earth. He is calling us to repentance with an urgency to understand our ignorance will no longer be an excuse. The punishments we have already experienced are but a shadow of things to come if we do not heed the call and wake up to the signs of the times.

Such [former] ages of ignorance God, it is true, ignored and allowed to pass unnoticed; but now He charges all people everywhere to repent (to change their minds for the better and heartily to amend their ways, with abhorrence of their past sins). (Acts 17:30 AMP)

Let us not bow under our heavy burdens and remain in ignorance any longer. God is calling us to change our minds, amend our ways, and repent of our past sins. Give all these burdens of the past to Jesus and He will remove then and protect our children from this evil legacy.

Come me upon to me, all ye that labor and are heavy laden, and I will give you rest. Take my yoke upon you, and learn of me; for I am meek and lowly in heart: and ye shall find rest unto your souls. For my yoke is easy, and my burden is light. (Matthew 11:28-30)

Jesus stands at the door asking to be invited into our individual lives and into this country that we love. It's up to us to open the door of our country to God.

> *As many as I love, I rebuke and chasten: be zealous therefore, and repent. Behold, I stand at the door, and knock: if any man hear my voice, and open the door, I will come in to him, and will sup with him, and he with me.* (Revelation 3:19-20)

Haiti, Abide Under the Shadow of the Almighty

The Bible is God's Word to us. He has written so many love letters to us. He has expressed His desire for us to dwell in safety under the shadow of His wings. He has promised to be our refuge and our deliverer if we would but call upon His Name.

He that dwelled in the secret place of the most high shall abide under the shadow of the almighty.

I will say of the Lord, He is my refuge and my fortress: my God; in him will I trust. Surely he shall deliver thee from

We need to realize that there is nothing in this world that can impede our progress if we are under His protection.

the snare of the fowler, and from the noisome pestilence. He shall cover thee with his feathers, and under his wings shalt thou trust: his truth shall be thy shield and bucker.

Thou shalt not be afraid for the terror by night; nor for the pestilence that walked in darkness; nor for the destruction that waseth at noonday. A thousand shall fall at thy side, and ten thousand at thy right hand; but it shall not come nigh thee. Only with thine eyes shalt thou behold and see the reward of wicked.

Because thou hast made the Lord, which is my refuge, even the most high, thy habitation; there shall no evil befall thee, neither shall any plague come nigh thy dwelling. For he shall give his angels charge over thee, to keep thee in all thy ways. They shall bear thee up in their hands, lest thou dash thy foot against a stone. Thou shalt tread upon the lion and adder: the young lion and the dragon shalt thou trample under feet.

Because he hath set his love upon me, therefore will I deliver him: I will set him on high, because he hath known my name. He shall call upon me, and I will answer him: I will be with him in trouble; I will deliver him, and honor him. With long life will I satisfy him, and show him my salvation. (Psalm 91)

We need to realize that there is nothing in this world that can impede our progress if we are under His protection. The Bible says in Romans 8:31, "What then shall we say to all this? If God is for us, who can be against us? Who can be our foe, if God is on our side?" (AMP). While God is for us, and we keep in His love, we may with holy boldness defy all the powers of darkness.

Isaiah 54:17 says, "But no weapon that is formed against you shall prosper, and every tongue that shall rise against you in judgment you shall show to be in the wrong. This peace, righteousness, security, triumph over opposition is the heritage of the servants of the Lord [those in whom the ideal Servant of the Lord is reproduced]; this is the righteousness or the vindication which they obtain from Me [this is that which I impart to them as their justification], says the Lord" (AMP).

Jesus said we do not have to fear anything that Satan, our enemy tries to throw at us once we are under the protection of the Almighty. "Behold I give unto you power to tread on serpents and all the power of the enemy; and nothing can harm you" (Luke 10:19).

People of Haiti, let's take what we have learned and raise Psalm 24 over all false gods, their prophets, and over all false religions so that they recognize that the One who created the heavens and the earth, the God of Abraham, Isaac and Jacob, is the King of all kings and Lord of all lords.

The earth is the Lord's, and the fullness thereof; the world, and they that dwell therein. For he hath founded it upon the seas, and established it upon the floods. Who shall ascend into the hill of the Lord? Or who shall stand in his holy place? He that hath clean hands, and pure heart; who hath no lifted up his soul unto vanity, nor sworn deceitfully. He shall receive the blessing from the Lord, and righteousness from the God of his salvation. This is generation of them that seek him that seek thy face, O Jacob. Lift up your heads, o ye gates; and be ye lift up, ye everlasting doors; and the king of glory shall come in. Who is the king of glory? The Lord strong and mighty, the Lord mighty in battle. Lift up your heads, o ye gates; even lift them up, ye everlasting doors; and the king of glory shall come in. Who is the king of glory? The Lord of host, he is the king of glory.

Today, I am a living testimony of the deliverance that God has worked in my life freeing me from the bondage of sin and death and the powers of darkness. Therefore, I glorify God with all my heart and soul and share my testimony in every corner of the nation of Haiti.

Faith cometh by hearing, and hearing by the word of God. (Romans 10:17)

If thou wouldest believe, thou shouldest see the glory of God. (John 11:40)

For God nothing shall be impossible. (Luke 1:37)

Praise God in his sanctuary: Praise Him in the firmament of his power. Praise him for his mighty acts: praise him according to his excellent greatness. Praise him with the sound of the trumpet: praise him with psaltery and harp. Praise him with timbrel and dance. Praise him with stringed instruments and organs. Praise him upon the loud cymbals: Praise him upon the high sounding cymbals! Let everything that hath breath praise the Lord. Praise ye Lord. (Psalm 150)

Why must Haiti wake up and return to God?

➢ *God has promised He will forgive our sin and will heal our land. (2 Chronicles 7:14)*

➢ *We have gone for help to all sorts of people and spirits that led us further into darkness.*

➢ *It is time for us to turn to the Creator of heaven and earth for our provision.*

➢ *There is an urgency to understand our ignorance will no longer be an excuse.*

➢ *The punishments we have already experienced are but a shadow of things to come.*

➢ *We need to heed the call and wake up to the signs of the times before it is too late.*

➢ *God promised to be our refuge and deliverer if we would but call upon His Name.*

Chapter Five

A More Excellent Way

*See if there be any wicked way in me,
and lead me in the way everlasting.*
(Psalms 139:24)

Chapter Five

A More Excellent Way

Submit yourselves therefore to God. Resist the devil, and he will flee from you. Draw nigh to God, and he will draw nigh to you. Cleanse your hands, ye sinners; and purify your hearts, ye double minded. (James 4:7-8)

*H*aiti needs a revolution to liberate it from slavery but not the kind of revolution we had in 1791. This new revolution must be to free us from the influence of Satan through the power of God Almighty so that this country can move forward spiritually, economically, and socially. This spiritual revolution will allow the Haitian people to unite in one spirit and become one with God. Thus we can destroy this satanic system that the enemy has implanted and which hinders the prosperity and well-being of our country.

James 4:7 says we are to submit ourselves to God. That means we are to submit our understanding to the truth of God, and submit our wills to the will of His precepts, His laws and His way. If we submit ourselves to God, the devil will be forced to flee. The enemy has deceived us for many years. The time has come for the Haitian people to fight for their blessings as the people of Israel did in the ancient times. We can receive our blessings only at the hand of God. How do we do this? James 4:8 tells us it involves three things. We must cleanse our hands, purify our hearts, and stop being double minded. This verse infers this is something we ourselves must do. The Bible also tells us why we have to make sure we cleanse our hands, hearts, and minds.

Proverbs 23:7 says, "As a man thinks in his heart so he is" (NKJV). Jesus said in Matthew 15:19, "For out of the heart proceed evil thoughts, murders, adulteries, fornications, thefts, false witness, and blasphemies."

Where a weak head doubts concerning any word of Christ, an upright heart and a willing mind seek for instruction. It is the heart that is desperately wicked (Jeremiah 17:9), for there is no sin in word or deed which was not first in the heart. They all come out of the man, and are fruits of that wickedness which is in the heart. When Christ teaches, he will show men the deceitfulness and wickedness of their own hearts; he will teach them to humble themselves, and to seek to be cleansed in the Fountain opened for sin and uncleanness.[22]

The Apostle Peter asked Ananias in Acts 5:3, "Why hath Satan filled thine heart to lie to the Holy Ghost, and to keep back part of the price of the land?" The sin of Ananias and Sapphira was that they were ambitious and covetous of the wealth of the world. They were double-minded and thought they could serve both God and mammon.

> **Haiti needs a revolution to liberate it from slavery but not the kind of revolution we had in 1791.**

Isaiah 26:3 says God will keep those who cleanse their hands, purify their hearts, and stop being double-minded in perfect, inward and outward peace. Those who draw near to God with a humble heart, trusting in God for their provision without doubting will have peace at all times and in all circumstances.

Humble yourselves in the sight of the Lord, and he shall lift you up. (James 4:10)

Humble yourselves therefore under the mighty hand of God, that he may exalt you in due time. (1 Peter 5:6)

Humility is the opposite of pride. Humility allows us to draw closer to God because we know we need His provision in order to have victory. Humility also preserves the peace among us as we will not be tempted to fight among ourselves for honor, recognition, or greed. Pride disturbs and disrupts peace, and keeps us from submitting to God. We think we can do things our way and we even argue among ourselves as to what the right way is. God gives grace and wisdom to the humble. To be humble and reconcile with God will bring greater comfort to the soul than the gratification of pride and ambition.

I do believe with all my heart that God is just and faithful. Just like God used many other nations to bring us help after the earthquake in 2010, He will use whoever will respond to His call to bring the gospel to Haiti. It is time to begin the spiritual revolution that is needed to truly turn the hearts of our people back to God, our Heavenly Father so He will not smite the land with a curse.

Behold, I will send you Elijah the prophet before the coming of the great and dreadful day of the LORD: And he shall turn the heart of the fathers to the children, and the heart of the children to their fathers, lest I come and smite the earth with a curse. (Malachi 4:5-6)

John the Baptist preached repentance and reformation, as Elijah had done. The Jewish nation, by wickedness, laid themselves open to the curse. God was ready to bring ruin upon them, but He sent John the Baptist to preach repentance to them. None can expect to escape the curse of God's broken law, nor to enjoy the happiness of His chosen and redeemed people, unless their hearts are turned from sin and the world, to Christ and holiness.[23]

It is impossible for our country to receive the blessing of God without breaking the yoke of the evil that has bound us for over two centuries. The Haitian people must first repent and sincerely ask God to see if there be any wicked ways in us, and then lead us in the way everlasting (Psalms 139:24). Many countries have tried to give us a hand, but nothing has been resolved because the problem comes from within ourselves. We have some things to resolve with God before our country can truly begin to move forward in health and prosperity.

> **It is impossible for our country to receive the blessing of God without breaking the yoke of the evil that has bound us for over two centuries.**

Be Responsible and Repentant

It is time that all the Haitian people are made aware of everything that is happening in our country. We are responsible for bringing change from within and nobody else can do that for us. One of the things we need to understand is that God does not allow injustice. God said very clearly to the people of Israel when He led them to Canaan that if they practiced injustice, He would use the land to turn them away because it is impossible for God to live in a country where there is injustice.

We must unite to do justly in accordance to God's moral law. We have to learn to work together in everything we do for the welfare of our country and our people. If we ask Him, God will give us His wisdom through His son Jesus Christ. When others offer to help us the effort will not be truly beneficial for everyone unless we are united, and have truly cleansed our hands of doing the work of devil, purified our hearts, and set our minds on the things of God.

> *Therefore do not worry and be anxious, saying, What are we going to have to eat? or, What are we going to have to drink? or, What are we going to have to wear? For the Gentiles (heathen) wish for and crave and diligently seek all these things, and your heavenly Father knows well that you need them all. But seek (aim at and strive after) first of all His kingdom and His righteousness (His way of doing and being right), and then all these things taken together will be given you besides.* (Matthew 6:31-33 AMP)

What I really like about the people of Israel is that they even though they went through times of tribulation, they blamed no one. They looked at themselves and they saw the cause of their problems was within them and they returned to God.

> *And the children of Israel said unto the lord, we have sinned: do Thou unto us whatsoever seemeth good unto Thee; deliver us only, we pray Thee, this day. And they put away the strange gods from among them, and served the Lord:*

and His soul was grieved for the misery of Israel.
(Judges 10:15-16)

If we do not take what we have learned from Israel and stop blaming others and look at ourselves, the blessing that we have received from God and men will be wasted through the greed that will consume it. We must stop seeking to secure aid from others only to fulfill our own personal desires. Though we have received blessings, they have not brought us into peace and prosperity because we have lacked true repentance for the wickedness we have allowed to permeate our country.

> **Isaiah 26:3 says God will keep those who cleanse their hands, purify their hearts and stop being double-minded in perfect, inward and outward peace.**

Stand United

On several occasions I have seen the people of Haiti come together to achieve a set purpose though sometimes it has been to do evil. Now is the time for us to unite to do what is right in the eyes of God. He will bless us when He sees our hearts have turned back to Him. I urge all Haitians scattered throughout the world to unite to mourn at the feet of God Almighty, so He can forgive and heal our nation. Pray and ask forgiveness for our sins and those of our ancestors. We therefore call upon all those who love our country to join with us in prayer.

I the Lord search the heart, I try the reins, even to give every man according to his way and according to the fruit of is doings. (Jeremiah 17:10)

Since we are assured God has a plan for Haiti, we are organizing a major event on this theme: **"Haiti! Return to God."** God has promised us that if we call upon Him and seek Him with all of our hearts, He will bring us together as a nation and move us forward in His great plan.

*For I know the thoughts that I think toward you, saith the LORD, thoughts of peace, and not of evil, to give you an expected end. **Then shall ye call upon me, and ye shall go and pray unto me, and I will hearken unto you. And ye shall seek me, and find me, when ye shall search for me with all your heart.** And I will be found of you, saith the LORD: and I will turn away your captivity, and I will gather you from all the nations, and from all the places whither I have driven you, saith the LORD; and I will bring you again into the place whence I caused you to be carried away captive.* (Jeremiah 29:11-14)

So we ask for your help in a united prayer for Haiti that as we repent and turn back to God, He will forgive our sins and those of our forefathers. Agree with us that God will use us and His other chosen servants through this "Haiti! Return to God" event to bring many to the knowledge and saving grace of God and that it would bring glory to God. Ask God to help us bring this message to all Haitians, no matter where they are so it can become a blessing for all those who receive it.

Again I say unto you, that if two of you shall agree on earth as touching anything that they shall ask, it shall be done for them of my Father which is in heaven. (Matthew 18:19)

We can all unite and make a cry of repentance before God Almighty to snatch Haiti from the hand of the devil which is the key to prosperity in Haiti. Satan has used his power to close the doors of our country, but I want you to know the enemy is limited and will have to flee when we turn to the King of kings and the Lord of all lords for our help. God longs to give us the key to prosperity but we must join together and unite in prayer and work to see Haiti return to God!

I will go before thee, and make the crooked places straight: I will break in pieces the gates of brass, and cut in sunder the bars of iron. (Isaiah 45:2)

And the key of the house of David will I lay upon his shoulder, so he shall open, and none shall shut; and he shall shut, and none shall open. (Isaiah 22:22)

> *To the angel of the church in Philadelphia write; these things saith he that is holy, he that is true, he that hath the key of David, he that openeth, and no man shutteth; and shutteth, and no man openeth.* (Revelation 3:7)

God longs to give us the key to prosperity but we must join together and unite in prayer and work to see Haiti return to God!

A More Excellent Way

Proverbs 14:12 says, "There is a way which seemeth right unto a man, but the end thereof are the ways of death." We have followed the ways of man and allowed the enemy to come into our land. We need to get off the path that is leading us to death and seek to find a more excellent way.

1 Corinthians 12:31 declares, "But earnestly desire and zealously cultivate the greatest and best gifts and graces (the higher gifts and the choicest graces). And yet **I will show you a still more excellent way [one that is better by far and the highest of them** all—love]" (AMP). God will show us the way if we would but come to Him, repent of our sins, and ask for His guidance.

2 Samuel 22:31 reads, "As for God, **his way is perfect**; the word of the LORD is tried: he is a buckler to all them that trust in him." God sees the end form the beginning. Only in Him can we find the path to an abundant life. He will protect us if we

place our faith and hope in Him. He will teach us the right way.

Will you pray with me Psalm 27:11-14?

Teach me thy way, O LORD, and lead me in a plain path, because of mine enemies. Deliver me not over unto the will of mine enemies: for false witnesses are risen up against me, and such as breathe out cruelty. I had fainted, unless I had believed to see the goodness of the LORD in the land of the living. Wait on the LORD: be of good courage, and he shall strengthen thine heart: wait, I say, on the LORD.

How can we as a nation find the better and more excellent way so that Haiti will grow and prosper?

➢ *James 4:7 says we are to submit ourselves to God.*

➢ *We are to submit our understanding to the truth of God.*

➢ *We are to submit our wills to the will of His precepts, His laws, and His way.*

➢ *If we submit ourselves to God, the devil will be forced to flee.*

➢ *We must cleanse our hands, purify our hearts, and stop being double minded.*

➢ *We must unite to do justly in accordance to God's moral law.*

➢ *We have to learn to work together in everything we do for the welfare of our country.*

Chapter Six

Participation and Objective

Again I say unto you, that if two of you shall agree on earth as touching
anything that they shall ask,
it shall be done for them of my Father which is in heaven.
(Matthew 18:19)

Chapter Six

Participation and Objective

B eware! The spiritual liberation of Haiti does not depend on a single sector, but on all of us. We all understand very well that the problem of Haiti does not come from a single person, but from all Haitians who live in Haiti or in a foreign country.

We Are All Guilty

The prophet Daniel did not blame anyone in particular but all those who were Jews, starting with himself, saying: "I am in the same state." He was convinced it was a collective problem, like we have right now.

We have sinned, and have committed iniquity, and have rebelled, even by departing from thy precepts and from thy judgments. (Daniel 9:5)

Daniel took personal responsibility as I do now, acknowledging that God is always in need of a man who will stand in the gap for his people and his country.

The people of the land have used oppression, and exercised robbery, and have vexed the poor and needy: yea, they have oppressed the stranger wrongfully. And I sought for a man among them, that should make up the hedge, and stand in the gap before me for the land, that I should not destroy it: but I found none. (Ezekiel 22:29-30)

I do not want God to say of us that He sought a man to stand in the gap but He found none. Matthew Henry's Concise Commentary speaking of the condition of Israel when God spoke this to the Prophet Ezekiel says, "All orders and degrees of men had helped to fill the measure of the nation's guilt. The people that had any power abused it, and even the buyers and sellers find some way to oppress one another. It bodes ill to a people when judgments are breaking in upon them, and the spirit of prayer is restrained. Let all who fear God, unite to promote his truth and righteousness; as wicked men of every rank and profession plot together to run them down."

I echo this cry that all who fear God must unite and promote His truth and righteousness. I will stand in the gap for my country and my people and gets things started because God has promised He hears the prayers of the righteous.

For the eyes of the Lord are over the righteous, and his ears are open unto their prayer. (1 Peter 3:12)

> **God is always in need of a man who will stand in the gap for his people and his country!**

I am sure the Lord will strengthen my prayers and I am sure that the Haitian people will join the great cry that we must all push our country to earnestly seek God Almighty.

O our God, hears the prayer of thy servant, and his supplications, and causes thy face to shine upon thy sanctuary that is desolate, for the Lord sake. O my god, incline thine ear, and hear; open thine eyes, and behold our desolations, and the city which is called by thy name: for we do not present our supplications before thee for our righteousnesses, but for thy great mercy. O Lord, hear; O Lord, forgive; O lord, hearken and do; defer not, for thing own sake, O my God: for thy city and thy people are called by thy name. (Daniel 9:17-19)

To all Haitians who have a dream of real change for our country, we offer a different kind of revolution to bring about this change. It is not with guns or machine guns. We come in the name and the power of God, because "the weapons of our warfare are not carnal, but mighty through God to the pulling down of strongholds" (2 Corinthians 10:4).

Let's Move Toward the Same Goal

I want to share this revelation with all my Haitian brothers, and when the great day that we all wait for will come, we can unite to cry to the great God Almighty.

For we wrestle not against flesh and blood, but against principalities, against powers, against the rulers of the darkness of this world, against spiritual wickedness in high places. (Ephesians 6:12)

It is important that we are all clear that this is not a political movement. It is rather a spiritual movement, guided and directed by God exclusively. The work we all need to do is to free ourselves from the satanic slavery that chains us and prevents Haiti from prospering. We must know that there is only One who can help and He is Jehovah God.

The vision God has given me to help everyone participate and move forward with the same purpose and objective includes meeting with the leaders of all the churches in Haiti to explain the importance of this spiritual revolution, and coordinate the prayer and distribution of our plan and purpose to all Haitians.

Everyone is invited to participate in this great event. It is important that the vision is boldly executed. Those who participate must not remain silent but discuss this goal with all of our countrymen. It is imperative that we unite and put aside our ideological and religious differences, along with our political and social issues so we can truly free Haiti spiritually with the help and the power of God. We understand that everyone has their own concerns and we respect them, but our main purpose is to intercede for our country and God will do the rest.

> **Our main purpose is to intercede for our country and God will do the rest!**

We must embrace our purpose as united Haitians. We must love each other deep in our heart. We must love our language, our society, and our culture but at the same time make sure that what we say and do pleases God. Carefully read the conversation Jesus had with the Pharisees on the subject of obeying the culture or tradition of the people rather than the laws of God.

Why do thy disciples transgress the tradition of the elders? For they wash not their hands when they eat bread. But he answered and said unto them, why do ye also transgress the commandment of god by tradition? (Matthew 15:2-3)

Jesus told us we must seek peace with our God first and love Him above all else in our lives. Secondly, we must reconcile with on another and then our history will take a turn in the right direction. We will move forward with the presence of God.

Thou shalt love the Lord thy God with all thy heart, and with all thy soul and with all thy mind. This is the first and great commandment. And the second is like unto it, thou shalt love thy neighbor as thy self. (Matthew 22:37-39)

Jesus said, "Every plant which my heavenly Father hath not planted shall be rooted up" (Matthew 15:13). God will up root any "weed" that tries to work its way into our country, our people, and our culture. We must learn to use the Word of God, for it is written in the Holy Scriptures, "The gospel is the power of God unto salvation to everyone that believeth" (Romans 1:16). That's why I have all the authority in declaring today: "Haiti, my country, my nation, is free of this satanic contract, in the mighty name of Jesus and in accordance with what is written in Matthew 18:18, 'Whatsoever ye shall bind on earth shall be bound in heaven, and whatsoever ye shall loose on earth shall be loosed in heaven.'" Please agree with me now that this is indeed true for our country in the name of Jesus Christ and to God alone be the glory for this century and centuries to come. Amen!

Attitude for Success

I express my deepest sympathy to all families in Haiti who have suffered and endured hellish conditions that have caused you to weep. We have all suffered and we all need to intercede with the Almighty God for all of our brothers and sisters wherever they are.

I thank God for allowing me to be part of the campaign for the spiritual liberation of Haiti, and I am confident that Haiti will be freed. History will speak of what God has done for our nation. I urge you not to lose hope and continue to pray for God's will to be done here on this earth as it is in Heaven. He is even now revealing to us how we are to administer His Word for the welfare of the Haitian people.

We must also realize there is great power in the words we speak and carefully monitor what comes out of our mouths. The Word of God tells us to make sure our conversations are filled with the wisdom of God and not the so called wisdom of this world.

> **We must also realize there is great power in the words we speak!**

I say unto you, that every idle word that men shall speak, they shall give account thereof in the Day of Judgment. For by thy words thou shalt be justified, by thy words thou shalt be condemned. (Matthew 12:36-37)

The preparations of the heart in man, and the answer of the tongue is from the Lord. (Proverbs 16:1)

If we believe what we have read and learned then everything we say and do will be according to the will of God. Jesus said, "If thou would lest believe, thou shouldest see the glory of God" (John 11:40). Jesus taught us that what we bind on earth shall be bound also in heaven that is why I declare that Haiti is free from all Satanic influence by the blood of Jesus shed on the Cross at Calvary. I loose the satanic hold on Haiti that has been present over two hundred years and bind the power of Satan over this country in the name of Jesus. All those who believe and accept that only God can liberate Haiti, repeat the above statement now in agreement with me.

A man shall eat well by the fruit of his mouth: but the soul of the transgressors shall eat violence. He that keepeth his life: but he that openeth wide his lips shall have destruction. (Proverbs 13:2-3)

That's why I say we Haitians must be careful with what comes out of our mouths. Our words must be in the language of God. They must reflect the faith that we hold in our hearts that God will show His greatness to the world according to His righteousness. We must study His Word so that the words we speak are in line with God's plan and purpose for our country.

Matthew Henry's Commentary says, "The affairs of mankind are thrown into confusion by the tongues of men. Every age of the world, and every condition of life, private or public, affords examples of this. Hell has more to do in promoting the fire of the tongue than men generally think; and whenever men's tongues are employed in sinful ways, they are set on fire of hell."

Read James 3:6-18 and glean the wisdom God has left for us as we seek to move forward with our spiritual revolution to free our country from the bondage of the evil one.

And the tongue is a fire, a world of iniquity: so is the tongue among our members, that it defileth the whole body, and setteth on fire the course of nature; and it is set on fire of hell. For every kind of beasts, and of birds, and of serpents, and of things in the sea, is tamed, and hath been tamed of mankind: **But the tongue can no man tame; it is an unruly evil, full of deadly poison.** *Therewith bless we God, even the Father; and therewith curse we men, which are made after the similitude of God.* **Out of the same mouth proceedeth blessing and cursing. My brethren, these things ought not so to be.**

Doth a fountain send forth at the same place sweet water and bitter? Can the fig tree, my brethren, bear olive berries? either a vine, figs? so can no fountain both yield salt water and fresh. **Who is a wise man and endued with knowledge among you? let him shew out of a good conversation his works with meekness of wisdom.** *But if ye have* *bitter envying and strife in your hearts, glory not, and lie not against the truth. This wisdom descendeth not from above, but is earthly, sensual, devilish. **For where envying and strife is, there is confusion and every evil work.** But the wisdom that is from above is first pure, then peaceable, gentle, and easy to be intreated, full of mercy and good fruits, without partiality, and without hypocrisy. And **the fruit of righteousness is sown in peace of them that make peace.***

What must we do to see the spiritual restoration of our country?

➢ *The spiritual liberation of Haiti does not depend on a single sector, but on all of us.*

➢ *All who fear God must unite and promote His truth and righteousness.*

➢ *It is important that we are all clear that this is not a political movement.*

➢ *It is rather a spiritual movement, guided and directed by God exclusively.*

➢ *We must know that there is only One who can help and He is Jehovah God.*

➢ *We must love our language, our society, and our culture but at the same time make sure that what we say and do pleases God.*

➢ *We must also realize there is great power in the words we speak and carefully monitor what comes out of our mouths.*

➢ *The Word of God tells us to make sure our conversations are filled with the wisdom of God and not the so called wisdom of this world.*

Chapter Seven

The True Leader

I am the good shepherd.
The good shepherd giveth his life for the sheep.
(John 10:11)

Chapter Seven

The True Leader

Has God called you to be a true godly leader in Haiti?
What are the characteristics of a true leader?
What makes a man a godly leader?

Is it strength of moral character?
Are you a godly leader?
Servant Leadership!

*W*e do not become a leader overnight. If we study the leadership training God gives His called leaders in the Bible, we will see it is a process an individual must go through to qualify as a true godly leader. In Haiti we are facing a crisis in the realm of leadership because our alleged leaders do not know how to fulfill their role. They have never taken responsibility for the major national challenges our country faces. They convince us they are the leaders that we need to pull us out of the down spiral we have been experiencing, but when they are placed in leadership positions they do not keep their word. We find they cannot be trusted to pursue the best interests of our country and its people.

Let your communication be yea, yea, nay, nay; for whatsoever is more than these cometh of evil. (Matthew 5:37)

Only those that have the Spirit of God or the type of character needed to denounce corruption in all its forms are the true godly leaders we need over our country. History teaches us that when a country faces difficulties, God always uses one of His servants to bring a solution to the nation. His servant leaders are those He has trained to be ready to answer the call when it comes. They were people like Daniel, Nehemiah, Ezra, Moses, Joseph, and Paul. If we read the stories of their lives, we see how God personally trained them, often through their own personal adversity, so they would have the strength of character to lead His people out of bondage and into the land He has prepared for them.

In our case, there is not even one among the current leadership of our country who was once less than nothing and has come to be recognized as against this corrupt system. Many have promised to end the corruption but instead they become infected by it themselves. I would like to remind all those who are part of this vicious circle that there is a God who notes everything those who have come into leadership do.

They may think they are deceiving the people but they cannot deceive God and there will come a time when they will stand in judgment for what they have done.

For among my people are found wicked men: they lay wait, as he that setteth snares; they set a trap, they catch men. As a cage is full of birds, so are their houses full of deceit: therefore they are become great, and waxen rich. They are waxen fat, they shine: yea, they overpass the deeds of the wicked: they judge not the cause, the cause of the fatherless, yet they prosper; and the right of the needy do they not judge. Shall I not visit for these things? **Saith the Lord: shall not my soul be avenged on such a nation as this?** (Jeremiah 5:26-29)

For we must all appear before the judgment seat of Christ, that everyone may receive the things done is body, according to that he hath done, whether it be good or bad. (2 Corinthians 5:10)

The Spirit of God has begun unmasking all these types of persons and will continue to do so until the transformation of the Haitian leadership is completed.

Were they ashamed when they had committed abomination? Nay, they were not at all ashamed neither could they blush: therefore shall they fall among then that fall: in the time of their visita-

141

tion they shall be cast down, saith the lord. (Jeremiah 8:12)

Characteristics of a True Leader

By meditating on the character of a leader, and studying a man like Daniel, I finally understand the qualities required for a person

> History teaches us that when a country faces difficulties, God always uses one of His servants to bring a solution to the nation.

to become a true godly leader. First, a leader must have the fear of God, and secondly he must seek the wisdom from above. Thirdly, a godly leader knows how to wait upon the Lord. He will always seek to do God's will, His way and in His timing.

Proverbs 9:10 says "The beginning of wisdom is fear of the Lord: and the knowledge of the Holy One is understanding." Leaders need wisdom which is comprised of both knowledge and understanding. Knowledge without understanding is useless. Wisdom means we study to gain knowledge of what God would have us to do. We learn His laws and His way of doing things. Understanding then takes that knowledge and puts it into practice. A true godly leader is not just a hearer of the Word, he is a doer of the Word as well.

But be doers of the Word [obey the message], and not merely listeners to it, betraying your-selves [into deception by reasoning contrary

*to the Truth]. For if anyone only listens to the
Word without obeying it and being a doer of it,
he is like a man who looks carefully at his [own]
natural face in a mirror; For he thoughtfully
observes himself, and then goes off and promptly
forgets what he was like. But he who looks carefully into the faultless law, the [law] of liberty,
and is faithful to it and perseveres in looking into
it, being not a heedless listener who forgets but
an active doer [who obeys], he shall be blessed in
his doing (his life of obedience).* (James 1:22-25
AMP)

The human body is composed of three parts: *the
mind, body and spirit.* We have the ability to reflect
upon the social and material world around us. We
may even see that there are things out of order and
may realize there is a need for correction. But if our
minds are not connected with that Spirit of the living
God, our ability to truly bring about godly change is
severely limited. God is preparing all those that He
has chosen as leaders, just as He did for Daniel and
all of the Bible patriarchs.

*As for these children, God gave them knowledge
and skill in all learning and wisdom: and Daniel
had understanding in all visions and dreams.*
(Daniel 1:17)

*If any of you lack wisdom, let him ask God, that
giveth to all men liberally, and upbraideth not;
and it shall be given him.* (James 1:5)

As a leader you must seek wisdom from above, but not vain learning of this world.

Who is a man and endued with knowledge among you? Let him show out of a good conversation his work with meekness of wisdom. But if ye have bitter envying and strife in your hearts, glory not, and lie not against the truth. This wisdom descendth not from above, but is earthly, sensual, devilish. For where envying and strife is, there is confusion and every evil work. But the wisdom that is from above is first pure, then peaceable, gentle, and easy to be entreated, full of mercy and good fruits, without partiality, and without hypocrisy. (James 3:13-17)

Jesus compared a godly leader to a shepherd. He said the sheep will follow their shepherd who will have only their best interests at heart. The true shepherd can be trusted not to lead the sheep astray. He will make sure they are well fed and protected from their enemies. He compares a good shepherd with a hireling and instructs us on how to know the difference.

I am the good shepherd. The good shepherd giveth his life for the sheep. But he that is an hireling, and not the shepherd, whose own the sheep are not, seeth the wolf coming, and leaveth the sheep, and fleeth: and the wolf catcheth them, and scattereth the sheep. The hireling fleeth, because he is an hireling, and careth not for the sheep. I am the good shepherd, and know my sheep, and am known of mine. (John 10:11-14)

A hireling is doing the work of leadership for the money he can make from it. He really cares nothing for those he has been placed in leadership over. He overlooks corruption if it serves his own best interests. A truly godly leader is willing to risk ridicule and even persecution if it means he can better protect and provide for those under his care.

What is a true godly leader?

➤ *They have the character needed to denounce corruption in all its forms.*

➤ *God always uses one of His servant leaders to bring a solution to the nation.*

➤ *His servant leaders are those He has trained to be ready to answer the call.*

➤ *A leader's mind must be connected with that Spirit of the living God.*

➤ *A leader must seek wisdom from above, but not the vain learning of this world.*

➤ *A truly godly leader is willing to risk ridicule and even persecution if it means he can better protect and provide for those under his care.*

Conclusion

I take this opportunity to launch a general call to all Haitians everywhere to make peace and stop fighting among ourselves. We need to combine our efforts as a nation to show the world once again our capabilities and that we can come together to overcome our disappointments.

I beseech you, brethren, by the name of our Lord Jesus Christ, that ye all speak the same thing and that there be no division among you; but that ye be perfectly joined together in the same mind and in the same judgment. (1 Corinthian 1:10)

Let us prove that we know and have chosen to follow the Creator, the God of heaven and earth. Let all of those who have made the decision to follow Jesus proclaim our allegiance to Him so He will take us out of the quagmire in which we find ourselves. For the sake of our future generations, we join together as one voice to call upon the name of the Lord so those who come after us can enjoy a better life. May all that we say and do prove without doubt that we repent for the sins of the past and desire to seek after the one true God.

Remember the lord, which is great and terrible, and fight for your brethren, your sons, and your daughters, your wives, and your houses. (Nehemiah 4:14)

And all things are of God, who hath reconciled us to himself by Jesus Christ, and hath given to us the ministry of reconciliation. To wit, that God was in Christ, reconciling the world to himself, not imputing their trespasses unto them; and hath committed unto us the word of reconciliation. (2 Corinthians 5:18-19)

Have Faith in God

Jesus answering saith unto them, have faith in God. For verily I say unto you, that whosoever shall say unto this mountain, be thou removed, and be thou cast you in to the sea, and shall not a doubt in his heart, but shall believe that those things which he saith shall come to pass; he shall have whatsoever he saith. Therefore I say unto you, what things so ever ye desire, when ye pray, believe that ye receive them, and ye shall have them. (Mark 11:22-24)

Dear readers, consider this book as a key to help you unlock the treasures God has for your life. Learn to believe in the person that God has enabled you to be. Remove any spirit of doubt from your thinking. Always be optimistic about the success that you will win in everything you undertake because of the faith you have in God and in His promises.

But let him ask in faith, nothing wavering. For he that wavereth is like a wave of the sea driven with the wind and tossed. For let not that man thinks that he shall receive any things of the Lord: A double-minded man is unstable in all his ways. (James 1:6-8)

As of today never forget this phrase, keep it with you wherever you are: **"Faith in God is the key to my success."** Please make sure that your mind is in harmony with this thought because the Word of God says, "Faith cometh by hearing, and hearing by the word of God" (Romans 10:17).

Very often people are carried away by discouragement or laziness and allow others to stop them from reaching their goal. Jesus said, "Since the days of John the Baptist, the kingdom of heaven is forced, and it is the violent take it by force" (Matthew 11:12). The message is clear. We are to learn to fight to achieve our goals.

Dear Friend,

I thank you for being interested in this book. Do not forget me in your daily prayers so that God can continue to use of me as a tool for His service throughout the world. I also ask you please, to pray every day for Haiti.

Thank you, brothers and friends,
Bitol Odule Apostle

The Plan of Salvation

*A*re you prepared to receive the free gift of God? If you agree, you should pray to the Lord in your own words. If indeed you need help, you can use the following prayer:

> "Lord Jesus, I know I am a sinner. I know You died for me. I repent of my sins and I ask You to forgive me. Now I invite You to come and live in my heart and in my life. Right now, I confess You to be my Savior and I promise to follow You as my Lord. Thank You for saving me, Amen!"

Lord, I ask You to bless each Haitian indiscriminately in any country where they are located, giving them a different mentality in which You find them pleasing unto You. Make us glad according to the days wherein thou hast afflicted us, and the years wherein we have seen evil.

> *Let thy work appear unto thy servants, and thy glory unto their children. And let the beauty of the Lord our God be upon us: and establish thou the work of our hands upon us; yea, the work of our hands establish thou it.* (Psalm 90:15-17)

I thank thee that thou hearest me and may your blessing be with us from generation to generation!

This book was developed as a referential tool for all Haitians and friends of Haiti who want to see a real progressive change in our nation so we will know exactly the route to follow to ease the pain of this country who has suffered in service and bondage to Satan for over two hundred years.

Endnotes

1. Henry, M. 1997. *Matthew Henry's Concise Commentary* (Is 59:9). Logos Research Systems: Oak Harbor, Wall

2. Jamieson, R., Fausset, A. R., & Brown, D. 1997. *A commentary, critical and explanatory, on the Old and New Testaments.* On spine: Critical and explanatory commentary. (Ro 3:18). Logos Research Systems, Inc.: Oak Harbor, WA

3. Henry, M. 1997. *Matthew Henry's Concise Commentary* (1 Co 6:1-9). Logos Research Systems: Oak Harbor, WA

4. Henry, M. 1997. *Matthew Henry's Concise Commentary* (Eph 5:5-14). Logos Research Systems: Oak Harbor, WA

5. Jamieson, R., Fausset, A. R., & Brown, D. 1997. *A commentary, critical and explanatory, on the Old*

and New Testaments. On spine: Critical and explanatory commentary. (Eph 5:13-14). Logos Research Systems, Inc.: Oak Harbor, WA

6. Haiti Poverty and wealth, Information about Poverty and wealth in Haiti http://www.nationsencyclopedia.com/economies/Americas/Haiti-POVERTY-AND-WEALTH.html#ixzz1tFZjSp8k

7. Haiti Poverty and wealth, Information about Poverty and wealth in Haiti http://www.nationsencyclopedia.com/economies/Americas/Haiti-POVERTY-AND-WEALTH.html#ixzz1tFZjSp8k

8. Easton, M. 1996, c1897. *Easton's Bible dictionary*. Logos Research Systems, Inc.: Oak Harbor, WA

9. Henry, M. 1997. *Matthew Henry's Concise Commentary* (Am 5:1-7). Logos Research Systems: Oak Harbor, WA

10. Henry, M. 1997. *Matthew Henry's Concise Commentary* (Ps 127:1). Logos Research Systems: Oak Harbor, WA

11. Jamieson, R., Fausset, A. R., & Brown, D. 1997. *A commentary, critical and explanatory, on the Old and New Testaments*. On spine: Critical and explanatory commentary. (Mt 12:47-49). Logos Research Systems, Inc.: Oak Harbor, WA

12. Henry, M. 1997. *Matthew Henry's Concise Commentary* (Pr 16:32). Logos Research Systems: Oak Harbor, WA

13. Henry, M. 1997. *Matthew Henry's Concise Commentary* (Pr 16:32). Logos Research Systems: Oak Harbor, WA

14. Henry, M. 1997. *Matthew Henry's Concise Commentary* (Col 2:8). Logos Research Systems: Oak Harbor, WA

15. Henry, M. 1997. *Matthew Henry's Concise Commentary* (Dt 8:10). Logos Research Systems: Oak Harbor, WA

16. History of Haiti taken from Wikipedia, the free online encyclopedia.

17. Henry, M. 1997. *Matthew Henry's Concise Commentary* (Ex 16:1). Logos Research Systems: Oak Harbor, WA

18. Jamieson, R., Fausset, A. R., & Brown, D. 1997. *A commentary, critical and explanatory, on the Old and New Testaments*. On spine: Critical and explanatory commentary. (Ex 16:3). Logos Research Systems, Inc.: Oak Harbor, WA

19. Henry, M. 1997. *Matthew Henry's Concise Commentary* (Ex 32:1). Logos Research Systems: Oak Harbor, WA

20. Jamieson, R., Fausset, A. R., & Brown, D. 1997. *A commentary, critical and explanatory, on the Old and New Testaments*. On spine: Critical and explanatory commentary. (Ex 32:35-33:1). Logos Research Systems, Inc.: Oak Harbor, WA

21. Henry, M. 1997. *Matthew Henry's Concise Commentary* (Ne 9:4). Logos Research Systems: Oak Harbor, WA

22. Henry, M. 1997. *Matthew Henry's Concise Commentary* (Mt 15:10-21). Logos Research Systems: Oak Harbor, WA

23. Henry, M. 1997. *Matthew Henry's Concise Commentary* (Mal 4:4-Mt 1:1). Logos Research Systems: Oak Harbor, WA

For comments and suggestions, please Mail us at haitireturntogod@gmail.com or visit our website Odule.net